Following Christ

Sermons for the Christian Year

— ROBERT BEAKEN —

Sacristy Press

Sacristy Press
PO Box 612, Durham, DH1 9HT

www.sacristy.co.uk

First published in 2020 by Sacristy Press, Durham.

Sacristy Limited, registered in England & Wales, number 7565667

British Library Cataloguing-in-Publication Data
A catalogue record for the book is available from the British Library

ISBN 978-1-78959-082-1

Acknowledgements

Bringing a book to publication is the work of many hands. The author would like to express his most grateful thanks for the assistance and encouragement he has received from Mr James Service, the Revd Dr Jeremy Sheehy, the Revd Canon Dr Philip Ursell, Sister Benedicta Ward SLG, and Dr Tim Winder. He has also greatly appreciated the cheerful help and guidance he has received from Mr Richard Hilton, Mr Erik Sharman and Dr Natalie Watson of Sacristy Press.

Contents

Introduction

When we think of the Magi or Wise Men, we sometimes imagine three men on camels, solemnly making their way across the desert, carefully bearing their gifts of gold, frankincense and myrrh to present to the Christ Child. It is a familiar image, depicted on many a Christmas card.

In truth, we should do better to imagine the Magi travelling as part of a caravan: a whole group of well-equipped travellers on foot and horse, with guides, cooks, servants, farriers, and perhaps even a doctor, all following the star that leads them to discover and worship the Son of God in a stable at Bethlehem.

This image of a busy caravan of people journeying along seems to me to encapsulate much of the life of the Church of God, and especially that part of it with which I am most familiar: an English parish church and its congregation. In my role as the vicar, I am not one of the Magi, but perhaps I am something like an ostler, working to keep the caravan going. The cast of our parochial caravan keeps changing. We seek to recruit new people as we journey on, and explain that the star is worth following, and that there is deep joy—as well as blisters—to be encountered along the way. People die upon the journey, while others are born. Some join the caravan for a while and then give up. Others join and stay. Some people are cheerful; others suffer from depression, or are poorly for part of the journey. Struggling along through the deserts or over the mountains, the members of the caravan discover all sorts of things about themselves. They find they can take on new tasks and possess unexpected talents, and begin to see gifts and the hand of God in other people. The travellers are all individuals, but over time they learn to rely on each other. Sometimes the weather is fine, sometimes it is stormy; there are unexpected problems and disasters, just as there are unexpected acts of kindness and pleasures. The caravan continues its journey steadily onwards through all of these.

This image of the Church as a pilgrim people breaks down if you push it too far, but nonetheless I think it expresses something very important about our Christian vocation and way of life.

As I write these words, I am preparing to give thanks to God for thirty years of priestly ministry in the Church of England. I have been privileged to serve in town and country parishes in the dioceses of Portsmouth, Leicester and Chelmsford. I have never once regretted being ordained. From time to time, I have had to deal with some very tragic events and distressing circumstances: this is the lot of all priests. But if there has been much pain, there has been much more joy. The truth is, I *enjoy* my work, and I am profoundly grateful to God for entrusting me with my priestly vocation.

Like everyone else, I have made mistakes and have experienced disappointments and setbacks. But, as things have turned out, priestly ministry has been much richer and more exciting than I could possibly ever have imagined on my ordination day. The lesson I have learnt, over and over again, is that in the end, *God* is in charge—not me. The Holy Spirit, I suspect, has something of a sense of humour (and how strange that we are often reluctant to attribute this particular characteristic to God). I have sometimes discovered that I am rather bad at things which, prior to ordination, I always imagined I would be quite good at. Conversely, things which once filled me with apprehension have proved to be exciting and fulfilling beyond my imagining. One of these is preaching. I have discovered over the years that if words can hurt and distress, they can also be used to heal, nourish and inspire.

In thanksgiving for my thirty years of priestly ministry, I have compiled this book of sermons and spiritual addresses, which I hope the reader may dip into from time to time, perhaps in Lent, during a 'quiet day' or a spiritual retreat, or when prevented by illness from getting to church. The sermons are each of a suitable length for dipping.

The subjects covered are deliberately varied, and include the teachings of Christ, the Church's year, the sacraments, holy days, and one or two special occasions. Most of these sermons were delivered at the Sunday Eucharist in my churches. A few were preached at special services elsewhere. My listeners have ranged from members of a religious community—who might be thought to be especially insightful and devout—through to people who had come to church for a baptism or wedding, and who previously had perhaps not experienced very much of Christianity. One sermon was prepared for a service attended by families, children and teenagers. This is all a reminder—harking back to the image of the caravan—that we are each at different stages on our Christian pilgrimage, and that everyone matters on the journey.

Not all readers will find every sermon equally interesting, but if they are bored by one topic (which another reader, of course, may find fascinating), they can skip a few pages and try the next one. Returning in a few years' time, the previously uninteresting sermon may suddenly speak to them.

St Paul once famously compared the Church to a human body, in which all the different parts—bones, organs, muscles, etc.—come together to form the whole. I think this was a very insightful observation. My parishioners have sometimes said to me: "Oh, Father Robert, we couldn't have coped without you." The truth is, I could not have coped without them.

Throughout my ministry, I have been privileged to meet and work alongside some wonderful men and women, lay and ordained, in parishes up and down the country. Men and women who are regular in public worship, private prayer and Bible study; who faithfully get on with the practical work of running parish churches, Sunday schools and church organizations of many kinds; who help out in soup kitchens and hospices, and listen to people who have no one else to talk to. Men and women who try to bring kindness and renewed hope to people whose lives are bleak, or terribly messed-up, or suddenly beset by tragedy. Elderly folk, who have long lists of people's names, which they lovingly pray through every day.

With gratitude and affection, I offer these sermons to all who seek to follow Jesus Christ and to live out his gospel, day by day. I hope that the ideas and images contained in this book may cheer, strengthen and encourage us all as we journey onwards and play our part in the Christian caravan.

Robert Beaken
Great Bardfield, Essex

1

Advent Sunday

*Preached after the terrorist shootings and the Bataclan
theatre massacre in Paris in November 2015*

We are all still reeling from the images and film of the terrorist shootings
in Paris and cruel massacre of so many young people enjoying a night
out at the Bataclan theatre. Our hearts go out in loving sympathy to the
wounded and bereaved, and to the French emergency services. Revulsion
has led us to ask many searching questions. How could such a thing
happen? How in modern times have some people become so alienated
that they turn to terrorism? Some people have gone further and asked:
how could a loving God, if he exists, permit this to happen?

For myself, a lifetime's experience has led me to be realistic about
life on earth. With candour and regret, I expect us all to have to endure
suffering from time to time. It is naive or unrealistic to expect otherwise.
Sometimes, things go wrong in all our lives, and bad things happen to
good people (as well, of course, as to bad people, and to the bulk of
us who hover somewhere between the two). As a historian, knowing a
little about Hitler's Final Solution and the Holocaust, it does not surprise
me that later generations also get up to much irrational and sickening
wickedness. As a Christian, I believe that God originally created men and
women naturally good; but that this was spoilt by the Fall and by Original
Sin, in which we all share. I do not, therefore, believe human society to
be treading a path of inexorable Progress. Rather, I think that we human
beings are a complex mixture of good and bad, as is the society in which
we live. I also believe there is a great well of evil, sin, pain and wickedness
in the world; and that quite often we are all tempted and attracted by bad
things. We each know this ourselves, from our own experiences. God

gives us the ability to choose—what we call free will—and sometimes we choose wisely, guided by God's grace, and sometimes we choose badly, led astray by the devil. As St Paul famously put it, we often do not do what we want to do, and we end up doing what we do not want to do.

Again, I must stress, it is very complicated, because bad people can sometimes surprise us with acts of goodness, kindness and generosity. As a Christian, I believe that there is always room for hope.

If I am no longer surprised by sin or evil, pain and suffering, it doesn't follow on that I do not feel them or become upset by them, for I most certainly do. The pictures from Paris made me weep. Being a priest can be quite tough at times, because one sees more of the seamy and painful side of human life than people think.

Archbishop Cosmo Gordon Lang, who was an archbishop during two world wars —about whom, by now you have heard quite a lot[1]—had to deal with Hitler, Stalin and Mussolini, so he knew quite a lot about evil and suffering. In his sermons and speeches during the Second World War, Archbishop Lang never bound up the existence or goodness of God with an Allied victory, although he prayed for one. Had Hitler invaded Great Britain, Archbishop Lang knew he was on the list of people to be arrested and shot. Had this happened, it would not have shaken Lang's belief in the incarnation of Jesus Christ, his crucifixion and resurrection. In all likelihood, faced with a firing squad, Lang would have embraced these parts of Christianity more closely.

If there is a great well of evil and wickedness in the world, I want to emphasize that there is an even greater well of divine love. As we try to explain to the children during the Christingle service, wherever we go, whatever we do, we cannot stop God loving us. Today, Advent Sunday, we are getting ready for Christmas and for the birth of Jesus Christ, the Son of God, who came to share our human life with us: the clearest indication of God's love. We often talk about believing in God. We perhaps need to remind ourselves that God believes in us, his children, and that he has a plan and purpose for each of us.

And so, where was Jesus on that dreadful night in Paris? He was in the heads of the terrorists, working on their misguided consciences, begging them to stop and repent. He was with the dying, cradling them in his arms, whispering to them of his love, helping them to let go and to move into the nearer presence of God. He was with the wounded, filling them with his Spirit, trying to help them to hold on to life and to recover. He was with the emergency services, and with the kind passers-by and neighbours who offered first aid and shelter. Today, he is with the families of the dead and wounded, trying to comfort them as they break their hearts.

As I say, after all this time, I am still deeply upset by evil and suffering, but I am not surprised. I am not a pessimist, but a realist: evil and suffering are one part among many other parts of the strange mixture that is human life on earth. I wish they were not; but there it is.

There is one area, though, where I am an incorrigible optimist: I am left full of hope by the Child born in a stable at Bethlehem. If there is pain in life on earth, I suggest that there is also much more joy. God's grace is deeply exciting: he knows us better than we know ourselves, and he takes colossal pride in every single one of his children. Once again: wherever we go, whatever we do, we cannot stop God loving us. Let our starting point—on good days, bad days and boring days—be Jesus Christ: his birth, life, crucifixion and, finally, his glorious resurrection.

2

Christmas

I was once invited to join a group from the Church of England, including Dr Rowan Williams, then Archbishop of Canterbury, going on a pilgrimage to the shrine of the Blessed Virgin Mary at Lourdes in south-west France, which was celebrating the 150th anniversary of the apparitions there of the Blessed Virgin Mary to Bernadette Soubirous in 1858.

I had heard of Lourdes, but nothing had prepared me for the plethora of tacky religious souvenir shops in the streets around the 'domain' or sanctuary; and I must confess that as our coach made its way through the town centre, I began to wonder what I had let myself in for. Architecturally speaking, I found Lourdes somewhat dispiriting. The modern underground basilica felt cold and damp, and reminded me somewhat of a concrete multi-storey car park: I was pleased to emerge into the warmth and sunshine. The older, late-nineteenth century churches were all right, but were nothing out of the ordinary—France has many finer churches—and they were crammed full of noisy, jostling crowds, as was the grotto where Bernadette had had her apparitions of Our Lady in 1858. It did not help that after a few days many of us became ill—I spent a day and a half in bed, feeling sorry for myself.

So far, so bad. However, there were a couple of moments, which, quite out of the blue, moved and challenged me as a Christian in a quite unexpected way. Both, in my mind, were tied in with Christmas.

On the first morning, it was announced that we should be taking part in the service of the Stations of the Cross, where one walks in a meditative procession, stopping to pray at various points known as 'Stations', while remembering Jesus' journey carrying his cross along the Via Dolorosa in Jerusalem to Calvary on Good Friday. We were confronted with a choice:

either we could undertake the Stations of the Cross indoors, on the flat, or we could scramble up a steep and rugged hill behind the church, with lots of stony outcrops. It was difficult walking up, we were told, and even more treacherous coming down. Well, all the hearty, rugger types amongst the pilgrims made a rush for the stony hill, and in a weak moment I decided to join them. It did not help that I was clad in a long black cassock. The going was just as awkward as we had been told, and it had recently rained, which made everything slippery. So, we made our way up the hill and down the other side, me quietly thanking God that at least I had packed some sturdy shoes. The Stations took the form of various Edwardian gold-coloured statues depicting the story of Good Friday.

The Stations of the Cross usually end with the death of Jesus on the cross and his entombment on Good Friday. But here at Lourdes there was an extra station: the resurrection on Easter Day. The sculptor had constructed a scene depicting the women and Peter and John, going to the tomb and finding it empty. It was really rather well done, and one sensed that an especial amount of thought and prayer had gone into this station. The tomb was depicted as a sort of cave. The two angels were clearly visible. The women folk peered inside. Outside, one woman knelt on the ground, clutching a baby.

It suddenly dawned upon me that the whole tableau resembled another biblical scene: the birth of Christ at Bethlehem. Here was a cave-like tomb, hollowed out of rock. Christ was born in a stable, which was not a barn—we can blame Saint Francis of Assisi for that mistake—but was actually a cave beneath the inn, as any visitor to Bethlehem will tell you. Christ's birth was announced to the shepherds by angels.

The clever point the sculptor was trying to make is that Jesus Christ's life must be seen as a whole, for we are redeemed by all of it. If we are poetic, we might say that the shadow of the cross fell across the baby lying in the manger. We tend to break the Gospels up into little chunks for the sake of convenience, and miss the overall picture. We are redeemed not merely by Christ's death on the cross, but by all that leads up to it over thirty-three years. So today, as we celebrate Christ's birth, we must also remember that he was born in order to die upon the cross to take away our sins. But at Easter, we must not lose sight of the fact that he who died upon the cross also came amongst us as a tiny, helpless, vulnerable human baby, entering fully into our human life, with all its ups and downs, and did so for our sake.

On the second night, we took part with the Archbishop of Canterbury in a candlelight procession. Due to a mistake in timing, I got there rather early, and I found myself in conversation with a man who helped organize events at Lourdes.

I need to explain that there are always many sick people from around the world on pilgrimage in Lourdes. You see some of them in wheelchairs. There was also a special pilgrimage of cancer patients whilst we were there, many of them very gravely ill indeed. The man explained that back at home, many of these sick pilgrims feel washed up, useless, passed around from pillar to post like unwanted parcels. For a few days in Lourdes, nothing is too much trouble for them. They are placed at the centre, and everything possible is done to make them feel special, loved, and wanted. Religious services are geared to their needs, and there are priests and nuns for them to talk to if they wish. They are assisted by hundreds of helpers, who often spend a week of their annual holidays helping the sick at Lourdes, and who seem to exude kindness.

The procession then started. Perhaps a couple of thousand sick people were pulled in special three-wheeled bath chairs, holding candles, accompanied by two or three times as many people on foot, singing hymns and pausing for prayers. It all felt really rather cheerful. As I looked at them all, I suddenly thought of all the work that had been necessary to get each sick person to Lourdes, all the travel arrangements, special insurance, trips to see the doctor to get the all-clear to travel, supplies of medicines and drugs, arrangements for nurses and porters at each stage of the pilgrimage. I then multiplied these things by all the people I could see, all those candle lights, bobbing along in the warm night. I suddenly began to feel very moved by it all, almost reduced to tears. I had looked for holiness and sanctity in church architecture, and had not found it. Instead, holiness, sanctity and very evident love were to be discovered at the end of my nose, in the very people around me.

Once more, I found myself thinking of Christmas. Everyone knew the Messiah was on his way: but all their expectations were wrong. They expected the Messiah to be a mighty warrior, a Davidic prince. When he came as a tiny baby, many people failed to recognize him.

There is a message here about our expectations as Christians. Very often we can get our expectations of God and of Christianity wrong. We think that God should behave or answer our prayers in a certain sort of way. And when God does other things, which do not fulfil our expectations, because we have the wrong ones, we are left floundering, all at sea. The divine child lying in the manger brings us great comfort; but he also reminds us that God is a God of surprises, and he is not always to be found where we expect him. Instead, we can find God in some pretty unexpected quarters and in some unlikely people, if only we have the eyes to see.

Back to my conversation with the man from Lourdes before the procession began. All this love, care and prayer, he explained, is poured out upon the sick. What happens afterwards is up to them and to God. Perhaps at Christmas time we might reflect that something similar is going on in our lives. God sends his only Son into the world, born of Mary, in a stable at Bethlehem. Christ comes to each of us personally, bringing us God's love. He saves us by his incarnation and thirty-three years on earth, by his wonderful teachings, miracles and example. At the end, everything culminates in his crucifixion and resurrection.

Looking at you and me from the vantage point of heaven, God might perhaps say to us something like: "I have poured out all this love for you. You cannot begin to understand how much I love you. I have not even spared my own Son, Jesus, who offered his life in sacrifice for you. What happens next is now up to you."

3

Christmas Angels

If you are a regular worshipper here at Christmas, you may have noticed that each year I try to preach about a different aspect of the Christmas story. Throughout Advent I have had a curious wish in my head to preach about angels this Christmas Day.

I daresay you have all received Christmas cards with pictures of angels on them. We have warbled our way through 'Hark! The herald angels sing'. I have been to several children's nativity plays this year featuring angels. Quite often our Christmas trees have a little tinsel angel perched on the top. The origin of all this, of course, is St Luke's account of the nativity, in which an angel appears to the shepherds in the field telling them of the birth of a saviour in Bethlehem, and adding, "This will be a sign for you: you will find a child wrapped in bands of cloth and lying in a manger." And suddenly, we read, there was a multitude of angels, singing, "Glory to God in the highest heaven, and on earth peace among those whom he favours!" (Luke 2:12, 14).

If you think about it, angels appear elsewhere in the Gospels. The archangel Gabriel appeared to Mary at the annunciation. Thirty-three years later on Easter Day, in St Luke's account of the resurrection, the womenfolk went to the tomb and found it empty. Suddenly, two angels appeared, saying, "Why do you look for the living among the dead? He is not here, but has risen" (Luke 24:5). One random thought popped into my head: were they the same angels at Christmas and Easter?

I must confess to you that I am not entirely sure I believe in ghosts and ghouls and things that go bump in the night. In the course of my ministry, I have been called to several such supposed cases, but there has always been an alternative explanation.

I have no problem, though, in accepting angels. I cannot say I have ever encountered one, though I once met someone who had, and she said it was the most terrifying experience of her life.

To me, angels are simply another, different, creation of God. The trouble with many of us is that we do not have a big enough mental image of God. We think of him as a sort of bigger version of ourselves, often reflecting back to us the values of our own society and culture.

In fact, if we pause to reflect for a moment, there are no really adequate human words to describe God. He is the creator of this universe and all that is in it, and, for all I know, of many other universes beyond it. This is why I have never believed that there is a fundamental clash between faith and science. Anyone who claims that there is probably does not know much about Christianity, or much about science, or has an agenda of their own. We are all engaged in seeking after truth, wherever it comes from, and I have always thought it is good to ask questions and to challenge ideas, so long, of course, that we do so with respect and humility.

And so we come back to the angels singing to the shepherds, "Glory to God in the highest heaven, and on earth peace among those whom he favours!"

It is the claim of Christianity that this enormous God—the creator of the mighty galaxies, and of everything from an element to a mountain, and of you and me—did something truly amazing just over 2,000 years ago. He came to earth and dwelt among us, full of grace and truth. His only Son was born of the Blessed Virgin Mary in the cellar of an inn in Bethlehem, and was wrapped in bits of cloth and laid to sleep in straw in an animal's feeding manger, which served as a makeshift cot.

Nothing in the whole of our human life and experience is on a par with that wonderful event. I am reminded of Sir John Betjeman's poem 'Christmas':

> And is it true? And is it true
> This most tremendous tale of all,
> Seen in a stained-glass window's hue,
> A Baby in an ox's stall?
> The Maker of the stars and sea
> Become a Child on earth for me?

No love that in a family dwells,
No carolling in frosty air,
Nor all the steeple-shaking bells
Can with this single Truth compare—
That God was Man in Palestine
And lives to-day in Bread and Wine.[2]

The shepherds went into Bethlehem, and found the baby just as the angels had told them, and knelt before him in adoration. St Luke tells us that they then returned, 'glorifying and praising God for all they had heard and seen, as it had been told them' (Luke 2:20).

What, I wonder, would the angels say to you and me? They would probably tell us to follow the shepherds, and kneel ourselves in adoration before the Christ Child. We are to welcome into our hearts the truth that this child is the Son of God Most High; and we are to spend the rest of our lives freely letting that truth spread and percolate through us, guiding and nourishing us, until at the end of our earthly pilgrimage, we and the Lord Jesus are forever one.

4

Candlemas

2 February

I have long had a great affection for the Orthodox Church, in Greece, Russia, and so on. I discovered recently that there is a tradition among Orthodox Christians that if you have a baby—and it does not matter whether it is a boy or a girl—you take that baby to church forty days after the birth.

This is an echo of the story in today's Gospel in which we see the Blessed Virgin Mary and St Joseph going with Jesus to the great temple in Jerusalem forty days after his birth. The Jews had an ancient custom whereby every firstborn male—whether a human being or an animal—was understood to belong to God. You had ceremonially to buy him back with an offering. In the case of a baby boy, you had to offer a lamb or two doves or pigeons. The holy family, being poor, could not afford a lamb, so they offered two birds.

Then, of course, we have Simeon and Anna—two holy old people—who came to the temple, spotted Jesus, and realized that he was the Messiah. Simeon spoke the words that have become known to us as the *Nunc Dimittis*—"Lord, now lettest thou thy servant depart in peace"—but added some strange words to Mary, "and a sword will pierce your own soul too" (Luke 2:35), which seem to predict Mary's sufferings at the foot of her son's cross on Good Friday.

As they walked home, Mary and Joseph must doubtless have pondered the meaning of this and other events: first the shepherds with their tale of angels, then the Wise Men with their gifts of gold, frankincense and myrrh, and now Simeon and Anna and their strange words. It would have given them much to think and pray about.

In about the year AD 450, Christians in Jerusalem started carrying lighted candles in church on this holy day, which later acquired the nickname Candlemas. As we process around the church, our candles have a two-fold meaning. They remind us of the presence in our lives of Jesus Christ, the light of the world. Sometimes following Jesus is easy, sometimes it is boring, and sometimes it is tough. The candle reminds us that Jesus, the light of the world, is with us every step of the way.

Secondly, the candle reminds us that we are light-bearers. Our task as Christians is to spread to those around us the knowledge of the love of God in Christ Jesus. We do this by prayer, by our words and deeds. It is a sobering reminder that for many people in Britain today, the only Bible they may ever read is our faces.

Let me end with those Orthodox Christians taking their babies to church forty days after their birth. That baby is, quite literally, their bundle of joy, representing all their hopes for the future. They want, somehow, to share all that with Jesus. At the same time, for the parents and wider family, life has dramatically changed. They may be tired. They must now get used to many new things and to a new way of looking at life. Suddenly, they have a whole lot of new things to worry about. For the parents, going to church forty days after the birth is a way of plugging their own lives into Jesus and seeking his grace and strength.

Twice in the past week, people have said the same thing to me: "I have to get used to the idea that things do not stay the same, but that they change." That is true for all of us. Life constantly changes. Candlemas and the little flickering candle remind us that the one person who never changes, who is always dependable, whose love for us never wavers, is Jesus Christ.

5

The Silent Years

We sometimes refer to the years between Jesus' birth at Bethlehem and his baptism by John the Baptist as the 'silent years'. This is because, apart from the incident when Mary and Joseph lost the boy Jesus in Jerusalem and later found him asking difficult questions in the temple, we know nothing of Jesus' early life. He grew up in Nazareth, became a carpenter like Joseph and then, aged thirty, he emerged into the public eye and began his three years of ministry.

What went on during the 'silent years'? Well, obviously, Jesus grew from a boy into a man. It is impossible for us to know with certainty very much about Christ's self-consciousness and thought processes. He was, as we know, both perfectly divine and perfectly human. One may speculate that as Jesus' physical body developed and matured over the years, so also did his mind. Jesus was brought up by Mary and Joseph to be a faithful Jewish man. He studied the Hebrew Bible (our Old Testament), worshipped in the temple in Jerusalem and in local synagogues, prayed and meditated. We may imagine that, guided by the Holy Spirit during these 'silent years', Jesus formulated the marvellous teachings of which we read in the Gospels—the Beatitudes, the Parables and so on—which God the Father wished him to teach to humanity. Finally, one day, Jesus was ready to shut up the carpenter's shop and begin his public ministry.

All of this, we may imagine, was a very lengthy and gradual process over thirty years. The Blessed Virgin Mary knew that her son Jesus was special: we read that after the shepherds had spoken of the message of the angels and worshipped the Christ Child in the stable at Bethlehem, Mary 'treasured all these words and pondered them in her heart' (Luke 2:19). His stepfather, St Joseph, also knew that Jesus was special. But to the bulk of the residents of Nazareth, he was simply the carpenter who had made their doors and repaired their furniture, no different from anybody else. So it was that when Jesus returned to Nazareth a year or so after beginning his public ministry, his visit was unsuccessful. If he had been an actor, we should have said that he 'fell flat'. On the Sabbath he began teaching in the synagogue. Elsewhere, his preaching had attracted large crowds, but here in Nazareth the response was 'Who does he think *he* is?' St Mark writes in his Gospel:

> They said, 'Where did this man get all this? What is this wisdom that has been given to him? What deeds of power are being done by his hands! Is not this the carpenter, the son of Mary and brother of James and Joses and Judas and Simon, and are not his sisters here with us?' And they took offence at him.
>
> Then Jesus said to them 'Prophets are not without honour, except in their home town and among their own kin, and in their own house.' And he could do no deed of power there, except that he laid his hands on a few sick people and cured them. And he was amazed at their unbelief.
>
> *Mark 6:2–6*

The people of Nazareth simply did not want to believe. Perhaps it was too much of a mental leap for them. They had pigeon-holed Jesus in a certain category—carpenter, son of a carpenter—and that was that.

Firstly, this tells us something very important about the nature of Christian belief. We shall not have faith in God if we do not wish to believe. Faith is a bit like falling in love: we've got to *want* to love someone, consciously or unconsciously. If we make up our minds from the outset that a particular man or woman is loathsome, ugly or irritating, then, whatever he or she does, we are unlikely to fall in love with them. Not unless—and I have sometimes seen this happen—we change our attitude and see that person in a new light. Likewise, if we decide, for whatever reason, that we do not wish to believe in God, then we will not believe. We will probably make the evidence fit our preconceived position: we will think only of death, pain and suffering, of hypocritical Christians, of the Church's mistakes down the ages. We will ignore the Bible, the sacraments, goodness, holiness, self-sacrifice, human forgiveness (let alone divine), answered prayers, the special atmosphere of holy places, and so on. None of this suits us. We do not want it to. But God, like a wise parent, is infinitely patient and full of love for his children. Things may perhaps be different later in our lives, and we may possibly begin to see Christianity differently.

The nature of God is that he never forces himself upon us. God always gives us a choice: to believe or not to believe. He gives us plenty of signs to lead us to him, but he never obliges us to have faith, for that would not be faith, which must be freely chosen. He patiently waits, ready to fill our hearts and lives with his love, whenever we turn to him in faith and love.

Secondly, the people of Nazareth are a warning to all Christians. They were not necessarily bad men and women. They were probably faithful Jews, in their own way; but they were blinkered and set in their ways. They did not recognize the Messiah when he came. We too can become like that, stuck in a rut, thinking we know all there is to know about Christianity, unwilling to do anything new to deepen our faith and commitment if it does not suit us. And like the people of Nazareth, we may miss God when he comes or calls to us.

After Jesus' disappointing experience in Nazareth, things fortunately improved. Jesus left Nazareth, and shortly afterwards he sent out his disciples in pairs. They travelled around the locality, preaching and healing, and had astounding success. 'So they went out and proclaimed that all should repent. They cast out many demons, and anointed with oil many who were sick and cured them' (Mark 6:12–13). There is a sense of excitement in these words: men, led by God, are doing great things. None of them had previously dreamt that *they* would be preaching, casting out demons, and healing the sick: all of which were signs of the advent of the Messiah. The message is to trust God, and to allow him to lead us into the unfamiliar.

What I long to do is to share with people just how exciting being a Christian is! Recollect for a moment what Jesus Christ means to you. Think of his love; of the forgiveness from sins he offers us; think what it means each day to know that he is guiding us, surrounding us with the Holy Spirit, whatever may happen; think of our hope of heaven.

Now imagine someone who has none of that. Think how marvellous it would be to introduce that person to Jesus Christ and give them all those good things. Think how their life would change for the better, and how they would blossom. Evangelism—spreading the gospel—starts with us and our own daily relationship with Jesus. If we consciously share our lives with Jesus, he will use us in his service, whether we are aware of it or not. And the first step is to admit frankly—and, I hope, joyfully—just how much Jesus means to us, day by day.

6

Come, follow me

I remember once sitting through a sermon in the 1980s in which the preacher told us with great seriousness that he did not believe in love at first sight. These things are complicated, but, thirty years later, I am not entirely disposed to agree with him. I think that sometimes love at first sight can and does happen.

Think, for a minute, of the opposite. We all, I am sorry to say, have had the experience of taking an instant dislike to some people. We tell ourselves that they are shifty, unpleasant, untruthful, stabbers-in-the-back, and so on. We may be entirely right—or we may have been prejudiced, or got off on the wrong foot with them, and misjudged them entirely. The challenge to us as Christians is to remember that we, and all men and women, are a great mixture of good and bad, of strengths, weaknesses and wounds. We must try to persevere with the people we find difficult, to avoid demonizing them in our minds, and remind ourselves that God loves them, even if we still sometimes find them rather difficult.

Back to love at first sight. If we have all taken an instant dislike to some people, there are other people whom we find instantly agreeable or attractive. A psychologist would say that we are each preconditioned to find a few people hugely attractive. Now, as soon as I say that, we all start thinking in terms of romantic encounters, leading to wedding bells.

But, there are all sorts of other people with whom we immediately hit it off the first time we meet: think of new friends, teachers who have inspired us, people in the same regiment, colleagues at work, and so on. You meet someone and immediately 'click'. You form what becomes a deep friendship. You find you can talk about anything. You do your best to help each other. Over the years, you have an effect upon each other's characters. You may not see each other for a very long time, but when you do meet, you pick up where you left off, and it is as though you saw one another yesterday.

Now, I tell you nothing new, and nothing that is strange to any of us. This is a universal part of human life. I mention it because it seems to me that it is the key to understanding the story of Jesus calling his disciples in today's Gospel (John 1:43–51).

There were some people who hated Jesus with a deep loathing: think of some of the Pharisees and Sadducees we read of in the Gospels, as well as the religious establishment in Jerusalem. Some people were indifferent to Jesus. Others went to see him because they wanted healing, or just for a lark. Some people went to see Jesus, met him and instantly hit it off.

Jesus, after his baptism by John, went to Galilee. He began to seek out the little group of a dozen men whom we know as his disciples, the people who followed him. The first of these were Andrew and Simon Peter, and then he found Philip, their cousin, and said to him, "Follow me." Philip did so, and the next day he introduced Nathanael to Jesus, saying "We have found him about whom Moses in the law and also the prophets wrote, Jesus son of Joseph from Nazareth" (John 1:45). Nathanael was at first inclined to be a bit dismissive, but he had a conversation with Jesus and was instantly captivated: "Rabbi, you are the Son of God!" he exclaimed, "You are the King of Israel!" (v. 49).

The amazing thing is that both Philip and Nathanael left everything and followed Jesus, in much the same way that Andrew and Peter had left their fishing boats and nets a few days earlier and begun to follow him. You sense that there was an immediate attraction in Jesus. They barely knew him—they certainly did not know how the story was going to unfold—and yet they realized that this man mattered more than anything else, that his invitation to follow him was precious and had to be accepted immediately. With the benefit of hindsight, we might say that in deciding to follow Jesus, Philip and Nathanael, Andrew and Peter had handed Jesus a blank cheque, to use them and their lives as he knew best.

Jesus calls out to us, too, "Follow me." We each have our own story to tell, and no two Christians are the same. Yet Jesus calls out to each and all of us, "Follow me", because he wants us to enjoy a unique and special relationship with him. He died on the cross, thinking of us. When we pray, we have his full attention. When we repent, he wipes away our sins.

At the end, after death and judgement, he will welcome each of us into the kingdom of heaven.

Our relationship with Jesus is just like that with our oldest and dearest friends. You find you can talk to him about anything, even embarrassing things: he has seen it all before. We form a deep friendship with Jesus: he is our Saviour, and also our brother. We listen to what he says when we pray. He does his utmost to help. Over the years, he has an effect upon our characters. Should things go wrong, and we fall into the snares of sin, and ignore Jesus, or are too ashamed to pray, when we eventually come to our senses and turn to him, he forgives us, and we pick up where we left off, as though we had spoken to each other only yesterday. Harking back to the beginning, the challenge is to remember that Jesus is also doing exactly the same in the lives of the people whom we find difficult.

Day after day, Jesus calls out to us, "Follow me." He calls to us when we are full of grace and sanctity. He calls to us when our sins weigh heavily upon us and we are all too conscious of letting him down. He calls to us when life is wonderful, and also when it is agony: "Follow me," in all of these. He has a plan and purpose for each of his children. Like Philip and Nathanael, Andrew and Peter, when we leave all and decide to follow Jesus, we offer him a blank cheque drawn upon our lives. If that sounds frightening, we may—to continue the analogy—imagine Jesus reaching out to take our blank cheque, with the mark of the nails still in his hands, the mark of crucifixion, willingly accepted and undergone, out of love for each of us. In Christ's hands, we are eternally safe and find our true fulfilment.

7

Seeing Clearly

Recently, I was immensely pleased to receive an invitation to help a small charity called the Ridley Eye Foundation. This supports surgeons performing cataract operations in the developing world and is named after Sir Harold Ridley, who performed the very first intra-ocular lens surgery for cataracts on 29 November 1949. Since then, 100 million cataract operations have been carried out. After cataract surgery, a fisherman or farmer, for example, who may have been losing his eyesight over many years, is suddenly enabled to see once again. He can do his work, put food on the table and care for his family. It really is wonderful. I find, therefore, that I tend to take anything to do with eyes just that bit more seriously in consequence.

In today's Gospel (John 9:1–41) we read about a blind man, who was reduced to begging. The men and women whom the Ridley Eye Foundation helps have all *become* blind. That is to say, they could all once see, but then they started losing their eyesight. The man in the Gospel is quite different: he was *born* blind. He had never been able to see.

As Jesus was walking through Jerusalem one day, his attention was drawn to this poor man. It is interesting to note that of his own accord, Jesus went over to the blind man. The contrast is with the healing of Blind Bartimaeus, who cried out and attracted Jesus' attention. Here, the Lord, moved with compassion, went over to the blind man to help him. Jesus mixed his saliva with soil, and applied this to the man's eyes. Saliva was believed to have curative properties. He told the blind man to go to the pool of Siloam and wash it all off his face. As the man washed his eyes, he found—miraculously—that he could see. Not see again; but see for the first time. Just think how wonderful that must have been for him; and yet also what a shock to his system. He had to get used to seeing things for the first time, learning what they were, distinguishing expressions on people's faces, learning to cope with the glare of the sun, the shadows at dusk, and so on. I daresay he was quite dizzy with it all, and yet hugely excited and happy.

Some people, though, were not excited and happy: the Pharisees, the strict, legalistic Jews. They were not too bothered about the man being healed. They were bothered that Jesus had healed the man on the Sabbath. In their view, mixing saliva with soil and putting it on the blind man's eyes counted as work, and so broke the Jewish law forbidding work on the Sabbath.

The Pharisees summoned the formerly blind man to their court. There was a great argument, and the man did not help matters by saying he thought that Jesus was a prophet. This, of course, was not at all what the Pharisees wanted to hear; so they summoned the man's parents, and tried to get them to admit that there was something fishy about it all. The poor, terrified parents simply confirmed that their son had been born blind, and added that they did not know how he had come by his sight.

The Pharisees called back the man, and told him, "Give glory to God! We know this man [Jesus] is a sinner", (i.e. because he healed on the Sabbath). "I do not know whether he is a sinner," said the man, "One thing I do know, that though I was blind, now I see" (vv. 24–5). This turned into a slanging match, with the Pharisees reviling the man, and him having a go back at them. "Here is an astonishing thing!" he said, "You do not know where he [Jesus] comes from, and yet he opened my eyes. We know that God does not listen to sinners, but he does listen to the one who worships him and obeys his will. Never since the world began has it been heard that anyone opened the eyes of a person born blind. If this man were not from God, he could do nothing" (vv. 30–3).

"You were born entirely in sins and are you trying to teach us?" cried the Pharisees, full of fury and pride; and they drove out the man (v. 34).

Jesus heard what had happened, and he sought out the man a second time. "Do you believe in the Son of Man?" Jesus asked him—in other words, in the Messiah. "And who is he, sir?" asked the man. "Tell me, so that I may believe in him." Jesus said, "You have seen him, and the one speaking to you is he" (vv. 35–8). Once again, Jesus states that he is the Messiah, just as he had earlier told this to the Samaritan woman by the well. "Lord, I believe," exclaimed the man, and we are told that he worshipped Jesus (v. 38). You will recall that *worship* is a very significant word, and one is only supposed to worship *God*. The man had gained his sight, and he had come to see that Jesus was the Messiah, the Son of God.

When you think about it, there is a lot of irony in this Gospel story. The Pharisees, medically speaking, can see. There is nothing wrong with their eyesight. The trouble is that in another sense, many of them have impaired vision. They have built up a wrong view of religion. For them, it is all about keeping laws, and we see their fury when the formerly-blind man contradicts them: "You were born entirely in sins and are you trying to teach us?" (v. 34). Like everyone else, they knew that the Messiah was coming, and yet they could not see what was under their noses. When Jesus Christ appeared, full of compassion, and healed a man born blind—all the things one might expect to see in the Messiah—they refused to admit the evidence of their own eyes.

The blind man was healed by Jesus Christ. He took a bit of a risk at Jesus' invitation—washing the mud from his eyes in the pool of Siloam, which must have seemed a pretty daft thing to do—but he ended up able to see. He turned it all over in his mind, and concluded that Jesus must be someone special indeed. Then, when Jesus told him he was the Son of Man, the Messiah, he worshipped him. We might say that he passed from blindness to sight, to insight.

A little earlier in John's Gospel, Jesus said that he was the light of the world. I expect we can all picture Holman Hunt's famous picture, entitled the *Light of the World*, in which Jesus knocks on a door, asking to be admitted. At the Easter vigil we shall light the Paschal candle, and then share the light, lighting the congregation's candles, and filling the church with light. This symbolizes the resurrection and the light of Christ dispelling the darkness of sin. It is a further reminder that the Risen Lord Jesus Christ is truly the light of the world. If we ignore Jesus, we can become like some of the Pharisees: medically speaking, our eyes may be fine, but actually, in what matters concerning life on earth and eternal life in heaven, we shall be blind, blundering around in darkness and refusing to admit there is a problem.

If, however, we grant Jesus Christ, the light of the world, admittance into our lives—if we open the door and bid him step in—Jesus will share his light with us, and, like the man in the Gospel, we shall begin to see things as they truly are. Like him, it will make us dizzy with excitement and happiness.

8

The Good Shepherd

When I was a student in Italy—a long time ago now—one of the places I used to enjoy visiting was the Catacombs, just outside Rome. These are a series of underground tunnels, which, 2,000 years ago, were used for burials. They were also used by the first Christians as hiding places during times of persecution by the Roman Empire. The Eucharist was sometimes celebrated in secrecy in the Catacombs by the persecuted Christian community. Walking through these underground passageways, the world of the New Testament and of the earliest Christians does not seem very far away at all.

The Catacombs contain some of the oldest examples of Christian art in the world. In the Catacombs of St Callixtus is a picture of Jesus Christ depicted as a young man carrying a sheep over his shoulders. This image of Jesus Christ as the good shepherd evidently spoke powerfully to the first Christians, who faced persecution and possibly death because of their faith in the Son of God.

In order fully to understand the significance of Jesus' words "I am the good shepherd", we must return to the Old Testament and to an incident which happened to Moses before he led the people of Israel out of slavery in Egypt to the promised land.

We read in Exodus 3 that one day Moses was tending the sheep of his father-in-law, Jethro, when he saw a burning bush; the bush was on fire, but Moses was puzzled to see that the flames did not consume its branches. He went over to investigate and heard the voice of God telling him to take off his shoes because he stood upon holy ground. God then instructed Moses to lead the Jews out of Egypt into the promised land. When Moses asked God his name, so that he might tell it to the Jews, God said to him "I AM WHO I AM." And he said, "Thus you shall say to the Israelites, 'I AM has sent me to you'" (Exodus 3:14).[3]

To the Jews ever afterwards, the words 'I AM' signified God Himself. There is a curious echo of this in St John's description of the betrayal of Jesus in the Garden of Gethsemane. When the soldiers from the temple reached Gethsemane Jesus asked them "For whom are you looking?" They answered him "Jesus of Nazareth." Jesus replied "I am he."[4] St John tells us 'When Jesus said to them "I am he," they stepped back and fell to the ground' (John 18:4, 6). Only after their first shock did they stand up and arrest him. Why were they surprised? Because, when Jesus answered their question, he used exactly the same words as God used to Moses from the burning bush—'I AM', in Greek, *ego eimi*. In unmistakeable words, Jesus was claiming to be God.

Now, this is where it all starts to get interesting. Seven times in the Fourth Gospel, St John records Jesus saying things beginning with the words 'I am': "I am the way, and the truth, and the life,"[5] "I am the light of the world,"[6] and so on. In our Gospel reading we heard Jesus say "I am the good shepherd."[7] When Jesus says this, he again uses exactly the same words as God did to Moses, *ego eimi*. The point is that Jesus is here revealing to us something of the nature of God Himself. He, Jesus, the second Person of the Holy Trinity, is a good shepherd.

How often have we thought of God as some great, terrifying figure; when in truth we could not have been more wrong? Jesus Christ is our good shepherd. He knows us and calls us by name, just like the shepherd knows and calls his sheep. How often have we thought that God was not really interested in *us*, in *our* lives? Yet our Divine Shepherd has been following all we have been doing with great interest. Elsewhere, Jesus tells us that the good shepherd leaves the ninety-nine sheep and goes off after the one sheep who has wandered away, and when he finds him, he carries him home on his own shoulders. We wander off into the ways of sin and unbelief, yet all the time the good shepherd seeks us. We have only to cry out to him, and he will find us and bring us safely home. A shepherd sometimes uses the bottom end of his crook to poke the sheep if they are naughty; and similarly, God sends us a bad conscience to poke us if we have erred and strayed. The shepherd also uses the curved top of his crook to pull sheep out of trouble or danger. Christ likewise comes to our aid when we ask him.

In the Gospel, Jesus then said something remarkable:

I am the good shepherd. The good shepherd lays down his life for the sheep. The hired hand, who is not the shepherd and does not own the sheep, sees the wolf coming and leaves the sheep and runs away—and the wolf snatches them and scatters them. The hired hand runs away because a hired hand does not care for the sheep. I am the good shepherd. I know my own and my own know me, just as the Father knows me and I know the Father. And I lay down my life for the sheep.

John 10:11–15

There is a strong hint here of Calvary. Jesus, the good shepherd, will not run away, but will lay down his life for us, his sheep, in order that we may be saved and have eternal life. This is important because it tells us about the love of God for us. Can you think of a better image of God than a good shepherd?

It is sometimes said that in the Church of England we learn our theology from our hymns. Let the last word go to a great hymn writer, the Revd Sir Henry Williams Baker. Inspired by Psalm 23, he wrote:

The King of love my Shepherd is,
Whose goodness faileth never;
I nothing lack if I am his
And he is mine for ever.

Perverse and foolish oft I strayed
But yet in love he sought me,
And on his shoulder gently laid,
And home rejoicing brought me.

And so through all the length of days
Thy goodness faileth never;
Good Shepherd, may I sing thy praise
Within thy house for ever.

Henry Williams Baker (1821–77)

9

The Pearl of Great Price

Preached at the Priory of Our Lady, Walsingham

A year or two ago whilst conducting a parish mission, I met a recently-retired teacher who was rather hard work. She had a bad word to say about everything, and on one occasion she took the biscuit by saying, "Aim low, that's what I always told the children in my classes. Aim low, and that way you will never be disappointed." I repressed the urge to say something in reply, and managed to turn the conversation into other channels. I wondered how many young lives she had stunted with this terrible advice. You see, I believe in the complete opposite: aim high.

In Matthew's Gospel (13:45) we find the parable of the pearl of great price. It may be of a pair with the parable of the treasure hidden in the field which precedes it, or it may be there by a piece of deft editorship. The temptation is to ascribe it a similar meaning to the parable of the hidden treasure, that is to say, to imagine a merchant who over a lifetime builds up a complete knowledge of pearls and acquires a collection of them. One day he comes across one of immense beauty and value—which he is able to spot by virtue of his lifetime of work and study—and so he sells all his other pearls in order to buy that one.

The deduction often drawn by preachers and writers is that the pearl of great price represents Jesus Christ, for whom we must sacrifice our all; a not inappropriate message on a day when we celebrate St Margaret of Antioch, a martyr who gave her life for Christ.

Well, that is all right, insofar as it goes. But the merchant's long years of labour and study leading to his knowledge of pearls can imply something of a hard slog beforehand. If we are not careful, we can end up with a false image of Christianity which echoes the title of Leni Riefenstahl's infamous Nazi propaganda film, *The Triumph of the Will*: namely, that if we grit our teeth, suffer, struggle and soldier on, then we might just, one day, by our efforts, find the pearl of great price.

It is easy to see how this parable appealed to a certain sort of Protestant Reformer. I suspect, too, it appeals to the Pelagianism which lurks inside many English men and women, and means that they seem happier trying to work their tickets to heaven, rather than simply opening their hearts to God's love.

There is, however, an alternative reading of the parable of the pearl of great price. In this, the merchant represents God, and the pearl stands for you and me. Not inappropriately, pearls are caused by an irritation. A bit of grit gets inside the oyster and irritates it, so the oyster surrounds the grit with pearl. We could, if we were minded to, see reflected here something of the Fall and of our Original Sin, which certainly irritates God, and the way in which he responds by surrounding us with his grace.

Just as the merchant has an extensive knowledge of pearls, so God has an exhaustive knowledge of his creation. He looks at everything, sees each of us, and knows our true worth. The merchant gave all he had to buy the wonderful pearl. Similarly, God gave his only-begotten Son, so that we might not perish, but have eternal life.

This leads us back to God's grace. Grace is one of the fruits of Christ's saving death and resurrection. Grace, in shorthand, is the love, forgiveness, strength and guidance of God, at work in our hearts and lives day by day. Grace is a free gift from God. Grace is not deserved or earned. Grace is freely offered by God to all. We receive God's grace in many ways. The sacraments are an obvious example; but every time we lift our hearts and minds to God, every time we resist temptation, or repent after falling into sin, every time we suffer because of fidelity to Jesus Christ, so God's grace is at work in our hearts. There is also a spider's web of interconnected activity by God in the world. There is a lot more going on than we can ever know or understand.

Now, I think I am probably a bit more inclined towards the second interpretation of the parable: God as the merchant and us as the pearl. It strikes me that the message is a little bit like that of the good shepherd who leaves the ninety-nine sheep to search out the one who has gone astray, or the woman who sweeps her house until she finds the missing coin.

However, I should not like entirely to dismiss the first interpretation of the parable. Having warned against an extremist, *Triumph of the Will*-type understanding, I must point out that Christianity deserves a constant effort on our part. In the old days, we should have said that God's grace was poured down upon us—forgive the image—a bit like custard from a jug onto a piece of apple pie; except that, to confuse the image, the pie had to sort-of reach up and embrace the custard. Some modern theologians have tended to see God's grace as something that is always inside us, and our task is to liberate it to work in our hearts and lives. It is the same idea, really, but expressed in two different ways.

At times, Christianity *can* be a bit of a slog. We must contend with the devil, who does not want us to believe in God; we must contend with contemporary society, which does not always much like people who have a different system of values and beliefs; and we must contend with other Christians, who can sometimes be rather a trial. It is all part of our vocation, to follow him who was crucified as well as resurrected. God's grace, though, is with us, around us and inside us, on every step of the journey. Indeed, sometimes it is the painful and difficult bits of life that seem especially to liberate God's grace inside us, the moments when, looking back, we can see that we have grown as Christians.

Whatever we do during our lives on earth, we must do the opposite of the miserable primary school teacher. We must aim high. A first-century Marilyn Monroe might have told us that pearls are a girl's best friend, because at the time of Christ, pearls were the most precious thing there was, far more valuable than gold. In God's eyes, you and I are the most precious thing there is. That is why God sent his Son into the world. Every time we pray—or suffer—we have God's undivided attention. He has great things planned for each and all of us. So, let us lift up our hearts, and open them afresh to the promptings of his love and divine grace.

1 0

The True Vine

One of the first things you notice when you arrive at Tel Aviv airport in Israel is a huge sign for the Israeli tourist board: two stick men are depicted carrying a pole from their shoulders, suspended from which is an enormous bunch of grapes. The vine—and thus the grape—was the symbol of ancient Israel, and the modern Israeli state has revived it as a national emblem. When Christ spoke about the vine, it had an immediate resonance with his audience: in our terms, it was a mixture of the English rose, the Queen's crown and the cross of Christ.

Jesus took this well-known and widely-understood symbol and adapted it to his own purpose. He said:

> I am the true vine, and my Father is the vine-grower. He removes
> every branch in me that bears no fruit. Every branch that bears
> fruit, he prunes to make it bear more fruit . . . Just as the branch
> cannot bear fruit by itself unless it abides in the vine, neither can
> you unless you abide in me. I am the vine, you are the branches.
>
> *John 15:1–2,4–5*

Imagine a vine. In the centre are the root and the central stem. The stem is often old and gnarled; it has seen many summers and many grape harvests. Spreading out from it are the branches which have been carefully arranged by the farmer. There is a great art to vine-dressing: you cannot learn it just from a book; it is the result of many years of hard work and experience. Every year the branches begin to grow, and the farmer has to prune them and train them to grow in a certain direction, so that they are sturdy enough to bear the weight of the grapes. He may have to thin them out, or remove them completely if they are growing into the wrong shape, but he has an idea in his mind of what the vine should look like so that it may be productive.

Jesus tells us that we are to think of ourselves as something like a vine. He is the root and the central stem, nourishing the whole of the plant, and we are the branches. His Father is the vine-grower. A human vine-grower begins by gently training the branches to grow in the right shape. He uses twine and wooden stakes to pull the branches in a certain direction. God the Father gently trains us to grow in the right direction through regular private prayer, regular Holy Communion and regular Bible reading. Our prayers are answered with hunches and feelings that we ought—or ought not—to do something, and afterwards we realize that God was gently guiding us all the time.

Back to the vine: sometimes the grower is forced to take more drastic action if the vine does not respond to gentle training and its branches persist in growing the wrong way. The branches have to be pruned and, indeed, sometimes cut off. Similarly, we find that the Holy Spirit sometimes uses the sad and difficult experiences of our lives to shape and guide us. It is important to stress at this point that God *never* sends us bad things: as a loving Father, he is incapable of doing so. But we all suffer the effects of illness, bereavement and of sin, our own as well as that of others. The experience of Christians down the ages is that if we offer our sufferings to God, he will transform them and use them to good effect.

As we go through life, we have to remind ourselves that we are being pruned, shaped and directed by an expert. Just as the vine-grower knows what shape the vine should be, so God similarly knows what shape he wants us to be, both in this life on planet earth and also in heaven. God wants us to share our daily lives with Christ—to abide in him—so that his love may reach us and that we may bear much fruit.

I should like to tell you a story about a young girl, Maria Goretti, who bore much fruit for Christ. I did not quite understand her story until last week in Italy, and I was profoundly moved when it was explained to me. Maria Goretti was born in 1890 to a poor farming family, who eventually settled on a small farm outside Nettuno, which they shared with another family called Serenelli. Maria had a very real and deep Christian faith. She went to church and prayed often. Maria was also a sensible child, who was sent by her mother to do the family's shopping in Nettuno. The church of the Passionist Fathers in Nettuno contains a beautiful medieval statue of the Virgin and Child, known as Our Lady of Grace, which was smuggled out of Ipswich to avoid being burnt at Chelsea in 1538 during the English Reformation. On her shopping trips to Nettuno, Maria would frequently pop into the church to pray before the statue of the Virgin and Child. Quite possibly from honouring Our Lady of Grace, Maria understood that sexual purity is an important part of Christian discipleship.

Maria's father died when she was nine, and her mother tried to manage the farm. In 1902 when Maria was aged almost twelve, the twenty-year-old Alessandro Serenelli, a member of the other family who lived at the farm, made improper sexual overtures to Maria on several occasions. This was plainly manipulative and abusive behaviour. Maria managed to give him the slip each time.

On 5 July 1902, Maria returned home from shopping in Nettuno, to find the farmhouse empty. Alessandro Serenelli was alone in the farmyard, and he tried unsuccessfully to rape the young girl. Maria fought him off and shouted at Alessandro that this was not what God wanted and that he would go to hell if he did not stop. The enraged farm labourer then picked up a sharp agricultural awl and brutally stabbed her fourteen times, before running away.

Maria's brothers and sisters returned home to find her lying in a pool of blood. They raised the alarm, and Maria was taken to hospital in Nettuno. The journey was long and hot. Maria asked for a drink of water, but the doctor thought it would make her worse and would not allow it. "Be patient," her mother urged her, "for the sake of Jesus on the cross, who suffered thirst more than you." Being urged by her mother to think of Jesus on the cross as her own life ebbed away may help us to understand what happened next.

The hospital chaplain administered the last rites. Maria was able to say what had happened. She then said of her assailant, "Out of the love of Jesus, I forgive Alessandro, and I want him to come with me to heaven." Maria is said to have spoken these words at the moment Alessandro Serenelli passed Nettuno hospital under police escort. Maria died the next day, 6 July 1902.

Alessandro Serenelli was tried and imprisoned for thirty years. Whilst in prison, he underwent a spiritual awakening, influenced by a dream of

Maria Goretti and by visits from a local bishop. Emerging from prison in 1934, Alessandro begged forgiveness from Maria's mother, who replied that she could scarcely withhold it as Maria herself had forgiven him, and the next day the two of them knelt to receive Holy Communion together. In 1947, Maria was beatified, and in 1950, she was canonized a saint. The ceremony was attended by her elderly mother and by her brothers and sisters. Also in St Peter's Basilica was Alessandro Serenelli, who ended his days as a lay brother in the Order of Friars Minor Capuchin.

As I said earlier, I have no doubt that Maria was the victim of manipulative and abusive behaviour. In recent years, many devastating stories have emerged of the abuse of young and vulnerable people in churches, schools, summer camps and in other organizations. Like many other priests, I have ministered from time to time to victims of abuse of various sorts. They have remained in my thoughts and prayers long after our meetings have ended. I commend them all into the loving care of God.

Many abusers are adept at covering their tracks and bamboozling others about the truthfulness of their victims, and this has made matters worse. Equally, one has to recognize that innocent men and women have sometimes been falsely accused of carrying out abuse by people who are confused, unwell or malicious. Their sufferings are very real, and they and their families need our support.

At the same time, I must record how distressing it has been to learn that some influential people in churches and other organizations have prioritized preserving the reputation of their institutions above helping the victims of abuse. As a follower of Jesus Christ, I find such an approach incomprehensible. As a parish priest, doing my best for my parishioners and for all who have turned to me for support, I feel badly let down by those who have sought to sweep abuse under the carpet. What truly matters is not the reputation of churches and institutions, but Jesus Christ and his gospel, and the people for whom he died on the cross.

Maria Goretti's story, involving the suffering and death of a young girl, is not an easy one. And yet I want to suggest that, rightly understood, Maria Goretti is a very significant Christian figure. Through her faith, Maria Goretti was part of the vine of Jesus Christ. We should never underestimate the faith of children. Who can doubt that Christ the suffering servant was close to this suffering child in her last painful hours; that his divine grace infused her, enabling her not just to forgive Alessandro Serenelli, but also to wish to see him in heaven. Maria Goretti, I believe, is a figure of abiding hope to all who suffer, or are abused, and to their families; for she speaks to us of the love and life of Jesus Christ, constantly flowing out from the vine and into the branches.

Let me end with a tale that the Passionist prior in Nettuno told me. Thinking of the life of Christ flowing from the vine out into the branches, the prior's tale seems to me to be a small but significant instance of how one intellectually highly-gifted person was moved by the life of Maria Goretti. A few months before his election as Pope Benedict XIV, Cardinal Joseph Ratzinger brought his staff from the Congregation of the Doctrine of the Faith in Rome to visit St Maria Goretti's shrine in Nettuno. After a while, Cardinal Ratzinger noticed that some of his staff—some of whom privately thought that they were pretty tough and had seen and dealt with most things—were looking at their watches and seemed impatient to be off to a restaurant as lunchtime approached. He began to weep, and said to them through his tears, "You and I have much to learn from a young girl who died forgiving her murderer and who was able to say, 'I want him to come with me to Heaven.'"

Fruit from the vine of Christ, indeed.

1 1

Confession in Lent

I thought that during Lent we should look at the traditional elements or ingredients of Lent. Christians use the forty days of Lent to have a bit of a clear out, and to focus afresh on what it really means to follow Jesus, in preparation for Easter.

One clue about Lent comes in the name of Shrove Tuesday. Now, this is not all about pancakes. The day before Ash Wednesday was the day on which people traditionally were *shriven*—that is an old English way of saying they went to Confession and received absolution in preparation for Lent.

This reminds us that one of the things we are supposed to do in Lent is to face up to our own sins and sinfulness. All human beings suffer because of the Fall and Original Sin. That is to say, we are all sinners, all of our lives. Only Jesus 'has been tempted[8] as we are, yet without sin' (Hebrews 4:15). In Matthew's Gospel,[9] we see Jesus overcome temptation. We, though, often give way to temptation and commit sin. Sin is something we do all of our lives—even saints—by thought, word and deed. Yet we struggle against sin, by trying to resist temptation and confessing our sins when they happen. We all have our ups and downs, but I have known lives changed and indeed completely turned around when people have repented of their sins and opened their hearts to God's grace.

One of the things we are to do is to examine our consciences, to tell God we are sincerely sorry for our sins and, if possible, to try to put right what we have done wrong. My advice here is quite simple: we should not minimize our sins, but neither should we maximize them. Trusting in God, we should be honest and matter of fact about our sins when we pray.

We have various opportunities to confess our sins to God. For example, we can confess our sins when we pray quietly at home. God is always pleased to hear from us, and *wants* to forgive us.

Again, at the start of the Eucharist and in other services such as Matins, Evensong and Compline there are prayers of confession for the congregation to say together. It is helpful if we can have a few minutes' silent prayer the night before, to remember the sins of the past week and offer them to God in our hearts in church the next day.

The Church of England also has the sacrament of confession to a priest. This is also sometimes called Reconciliation. Some people dislike the idea of confession but provision for it is to be found in the 1662 *Book of Common Prayer* and in Canon Law. Sacramental confession in the Church of England is not compulsory, but neither is it rare. It has been commended by such Anglican luminaries as Richard Hooker, George Herbert and Jeremy Taylor.

I made my first sacramental confession when I was a teenage student, and I have made my confession periodically ever since. I went to All Saints' Church, Margaret Street, near Oxford Circus in London. "I've never done this before," I said to the vicar. "Don't worry," he said, "say what you can remember, in your own words"—and of course, I cannot say any more, because what we call the seal of the confessional means that neither the priest nor the penitent can ever talk about it afterwards. I found going to confession a very helpful experience and have regularly made my confession ever since.

I did not know at the time, but the vicar who heard my first confession, Father David Sparrow, was terminally ill with cancer. He had dragged himself into church that day to hear confessions, because he wanted to help people. Two or three months later, he was dead. When I later found out about his cancer, it made a great impression on me: at its core, priestly ministry is about helping people to be reconciled to God and to know the liberating and transforming power of his love.

An idea occurred to me nearly forty years after the event: perhaps God used the first confession of this nervous, rather over-pious teenager to help Father David Sparrow at the end of his life. Perhaps hearing a first confession helped this dying priest to know that he was still wanted and still being used by God, despite his mortal illness, right at the end of his life. There are no coincidences where God is concerned.

Another point: if confession and forgiveness is vertical, i.e. between us and God, it is also supposed to be horizontal, between us and other people. God will not want us in heaven if we are 'daggers drawn' with other men and women. We all have bad experiences in life. Other people can sometimes rub us up the wrong way or treat us very badly indeed. But then, I daresay we sometimes rub other people up the wrong way, and we may not always have treated everyone well. It is very easy to harbour grudges and let resentments fester. We have to forgive other people: Jesus told us that the measure of forgiveness we give to others is the measure we shall receive back from God on the day of judgement. And you know, with God's grace it *is* possible to forgive others, even when they have badly hurt us. It may take years, and we may still never like them, but we can—with God's help—forgive their words and actions, and let go of the past. A member of my family was one of the youngest Allied prisoners of war in the notorious Japanese Changi prison camp during the Second World War, where he saw and experienced some truly terrible things. He told me he had managed to forgive his cruel Japanese captors. It took him until sometime in the early 1950s finally to let go and feel at peace, but in the end he managed to do it. He did not want the past to be more important than the present or the future. He went on after the war to be ordained to the priesthood.

Lastly, we have to learn to forgive ourselves. We all have sins, failures, wounds and things about which we are sensitive. Sometimes, we can feel very bad about these things and be harsh with ourselves. Over the years, I have had to learn that God is actually the vicar of the parish and not me. If my intentions are right, but, because I am overburdened with work or unwell, and consequently I do not get around to doing something in the parish, or unfortunately I do it, but not very well, then there is little point in beating myself up. I may have to learn lessons, such as pacing myself better or asking for help, but in the end, God is in charge. If he can lead a teenage boy into church to make his confession to a dying priest and to be profoundly moved for the rest of his life by that experience—and perhaps thu salso help the dying priest—God can sort out other things too. It sounds a truism, but we have to have faith, learn to forgive ourselves, place everything in God's hands and cheerfully move on.

As I said earlier, we must neither minimize our sins, nor maximize them. Confession of sins—however we do it—is a regular part of the life of every Christian. At a deeper level, confession is not just about repenting of our sins and receiving absolution: it is about humbly and yet joyfully offering God our lives—the very core of our selves—in worship and adoration.

Palm Sunday

Jerusalem on Palm Sunday in AD 33 was starting to fill up with pilgrims, visitors from far and wide who had come for the annual festival of the Passover. The population of the holy city more than doubled for ten days or so. For the shopkeepers it was a chance to make a fast buck; for the Jewish authorities having so many excited people crammed together for a few days was apt to be a headache, and there was the constant anxiety of disturbances, riots and a crackdown by the Romans.

Into this tinder-box rode Jesus on a donkey. Jewish kings rode on donkeys through the streets of Jerusalem to their coronations in the Temple. Jesus was here proclaiming that he was the Son of David, the Messiah, the Promised One. The crowds waved palms, shouted "Hosanna to the Son of David" and "Blessed is he who comes in the name of the Lord!" They put their coats and greenery on the road for the donkey to walk upon, which to them was the equivalent of our laying a red carpet for a visit by the Queen. Jesus went to the temple, but not to be crowned: he went to overturn the tables of the money changers, to set free the captive pigeons, and to declare "It is written, 'My house shall be called a house of prayer', but you are making it a den of robbers" (Matthew 21:13). The only crown placed upon the head of Jesus that week, we might remember, was the crown of thorns.

It is easy to be over-romantic about this entry into Jerusalem. Some of the cheering crowds were undoubtedly the followers of Jesus who had realized his identity, the Son of God. But others were just ordinary members of the public, pilgrims in town for a few days, shopkeepers, apprentices, and so on, for whom all this shouting and cheering was a five-minute wonder. They joined in for a laugh, and then quickly forgot all about it. Not for nothing does the Church appoint that I should read the Passion as the Gospel reading on Palm Sunday, after the Procession. The point is that it was the very same people who on Sunday shouted "Blessed is the one who comes in the name of the Lord," who by Friday were shouting "Crucify him, crucify him!"

And so, on Palm Sunday we enter Holy Week, which for Christians is the most important and sacred week in the whole year. If we hope one day to enter heaven, it is because of the events of this week, and it makes little sense to celebrate the resurrection on Easter Day if we have not first commemorated the crucifixion on Good Friday—the sacrifice that atoned for our sins.

In truth, instead of a lot of services, it would be more accurate to say that we have one big service stretching over three days. On Maundy Thursday we remember Christ's washing of the disciples' feet and his institution of the Eucharist; we recall his betrayal and arrest in the Garden of Gethsemane; and we keep a watch of prayer until midnight—along with Christians the world over—trying to atone for his desertion by the disciples.

On Good Friday we remember Christ's crucifixion. Our Good Friday service is very simple, and is profoundly moving.

On Easter Eve we move from darkness to light, from despair to inexpressible joy, for, as he promised, Christ is risen from the dead. God's love has overcome the very worst evil and is triumphant. That is the meaning behind the very ancient ceremony of blessing the Easter fire, carrying the paschal candle into church, and sharing the light. As the darkness gives way to the light, so we remember Christ rising from the dead, his victory over sin, evil and death complete.

On Easter Day we have our usual rumbustious Family Easter Eucharist: we need lots of hand bells to ring during the service announcing the resurrection of Christ.

There is a temptation this week for us to say to ourselves "Oh well, I know the Easter story. I've heard it hundreds of times. All we are doing is reminding ourselves of things we already know." Well, this is not entirely true and it misses the important point of these next few days. The reason I am anxious that we create time to come to church in Holy Week is that for a few hours the veil is parted, and we are not in our parish church, but we are *there,* in Jerusalem with Jesus. We are present in the Upper Room and in the Garden of Gethsemane; we are standing on the pavement in the Via Dolorosa as Christ shuffles past carrying his cross. We are next to Mary and John and the others at Calvary, watching Jesus die on the cross; and we are with Mary Magdalene in the garden early on Easter Day, meeting the risen Lord. Every year we see something new, some aspect of the Gospel which we had not before understood or appreciated. By the end of it all, we are nourished and transformed in some way or other, planned by God, and of which we ourselves may be entirely unaware.

Holy Week *is* challenging, but at the end of it we know that God loves us with a passion and depth we can barely imagine.

1 3

Maundy Thursday

When I was a student, by chance I got to know a community of Anglican Sisters, the Society of St Margaret at St Saviour's Priory at Haggerston in the East End of London. They played a big part in my life and in my spiritual evolution from evangelicalism to a more catholic Anglicanism. In recent weeks I have found myself thinking often about one of them, Sister Natalie, who was what we might describe as very 'top drawer', and came from a moneyed and privileged background, which in her youth she abandoned to join an Anglican religious community, and to work and pray among the poorest of the poor in Bethnal Green. She told me that had she not become a Christian, she would have worshipped dogs and the sun, but Jesus got in first. Sister Natalie was a sort of jolly version of Queen Mary, in a grey habit and black veil. As I got to know her and the other Sisters, I realized two things. Firstly, the Eucharist meant a lot to them: they had a daily celebration in their chapel as well as all their other services and time devoted to private prayer. Secondly, they went anywhere and dealt with anyone: no one was too dirty, too smelly, too horrible for them to try to help. I began, dimly at first, to perceive a connection between the two. I also noticed that the Sisters seemed always cheerful and happy.

Sister Natalie was well known and popular in the East End. She told me one morning how she had been summoned in the middle of the previous night to go to a woman in Bethnal Green who had gone into premature labour and had given birth to a tiny baby that was not expected to survive. Sister Natalie had administered emergency baptism to the baby and done what she could to comfort this young East End mother and her family in their anxiety and distress.

As well as a deep and very practical Christian faith, Sister Natalie also had a great and indeed slightly naughty sense of humour. On one occasion she went to see an old Cockney lady, who said, "I called me first daughter 'Maudie.'" "What a nice name," said Sister Natalie, "why did you call her 'Maudie'?" "Cos," the old lady replied, "she was born on Maudie Fursday."

Well, there is actually a letter *n* in today's name: Maundy Thursday. Maundy is an old English word derived from a Latin word, *mandatum*, or commandment. "I give you a new commandment, that you love one another," said Jesus. "Just as I have loved you, you also should love one another" (John 13:34).

Tonight, in our hearts and imaginations, Christians the world over join Jesus in the Upper Room in Jerusalem, to witness the Last Supper, the occasion when Christ gave us that commandment. It was a strange meal, and one that will never be forgotten as long as the Church exists to recall it. Something did not go quite right with the catering arrangements. The disciples would have reclined upon low couches around a central table, from which they helped themselves to the food. Their feet would have pointed away from the table, and it was the custom for a servant to walk around the table with water and towels, washing the dusty feet of the diners. This was an unpleasant job—imagine what they had walked through in the Jerusalem streets outside—and most people would just take the servant for granted; they probably would not even have spoken to him. Well, as I say, something went wrong. The food and drink were there, but there was no one to wash the disciples' feet. I suppose it is even possible that Jesus may have sent the servants away, in order that he might make a point. Jesus got up from his place, put a towel around his waist, and himself washed the feet of the disciples. In our terms it must have seemed as though the Queen put on an apron, waved away the footmen, and started clearing the dishes from a state banquet at Buckingham Palace. Peter's reaction was consternation, but Christ carried on. We might remind ourselves that some of the feet Jesus washed belonged to people who were shortly to betray him or desert him at Gethsemane, the feet of people who were far from perfect. As Jesus sat down again he explained what he had done:

Do you know what I have done to you? You call me Teacher and Lord—and you are right, for that is what I am. So if I, your Lord and Teacher, have washed your feet, you also ought to wash one another's feet. For I have set you an example, that you also should do as I have done to you.

John 13:12–15

But that was not all. Jesus took the bread and the wine, common, everyday food and drink, and he used them to institute the Eucharist. He transformed bread into his own body and wine into his own blood. I quote from the original Greek words in St Mark:

And as they were eating, taking a loaf, blessing, he broke and gave to them and said: Take you; this is the body of me. And taking a cup, giving thanks, he gave to them, and drank of it all. And he said to them: This is the blood of me, of the covenant—being shed for many.

Mark 14:22–4

I have deliberately used these clumsy words because they are a literal translation of the original Greek and have not been tidied up in any way. I have done so in order to draw attention to Christ's actual words: *This is the body of me* and *this is the blood of me*. It is quite clear from the original Greek New Testament text that he uses these words, *soma* and *aima*, meaning *body* and *blood*, flesh and the red stuff that goes through our veins. Not a symbol or a sign, but flesh and blood. In the Eucharist, the bread and wine become the sacramental body and blood of Christ. They are not merely symbols, but Christ is truly present in them, what we call the Real Presence. The Church of England has always refused to try to define the relationship of God's gift to the elements of bread and wine—it is a deep and sacred mystery—and Anglicans have stressed the importance of faith in the communicant. But, in the words of the Prayer Book, we are fed 'with the spiritual food of the most precious Body and Blood of thy Son our Saviour Jesus Christ'. In the words of one person at our Lent Bible Study Groups, this Real Presence is "awesome". It is indeed, but when you think about it, Christ gave us the Eucharist at the Last Supper so that he could always be with us: an act of awesome love.

Dom Gregory Dix, the great Anglican Benedictine monk and liturgical scholar summed up the impact of Christ's command at the Last Supper in his famous book *The Shape of the Liturgy*:

> Was ever another command so obeyed? For century after century, spreading slowly to every continent and country and among every race on earth, this action has been done, in every conceivable human circumstance, for every conceivable human need from infancy and before it to extreme old age and after it, from the pinnacles of earthly greatness to the refuge of fugitives in the caves and dens of the earth. Men have found no better thing than this to do for kings at their crowning and criminals going to the scaffold; for armies in triumph or for a bride and bridegroom in a little country church; for the proclamation of a dogma or for a good crop of wheat; for the wisdom of a Parliament of a mighty nation or for a sick old woman afraid to die; for a schoolboy sitting an examination or for Columbus setting out to discover America; for the famine of whole provinces or for the soul of a dead lover; in thankfulness because my father did not die of pneumonia; for a village headman much tempted to return to fetich because the yams had failed; because the Turk was at the gates of Vienna; for the repentance of Margaret; for the settlement of a strike; for a son for a barren woman; for Captain so-and-so, wounded and prisoner-of-war; while the lions roared in the nearby amphitheatre; on the beach at Dunkirk; while the hiss of the scythes in the thick June grass came faintly through the windows of the church; tremulously, by an old monk on the fiftieth anniversary of his vows; furtively, by an exiled bishop who had hewn timber all day in a prison camp near Murmansk; gorgeously, for the canonization of St Joan of Arc—one could fill many pages with the reasons why men have done this, and not tell a hundredth part of them. And best of all, week by week and month by month, on a hundred thousand successive Sundays, faithfully, unfailingly, across all the parishes of Christendom, the

pastors have done this just to *make* the *plebs sancta Dei*—the holy common people of God.[10]

It is time to return to Sister Natalie and Maudie's mum in the streets of Bethnal Green. I have said that these Anglican Sisters went anywhere to help people: no one was too dirty, smelly or horrible for them. They dealt with people who fell through the gaps in the Social Services and NHS and who had no one else to turn to. In their lives, we see reflected the unity of the two parts of the Last Supper when Christ instituted the Eucharist. He comes to us in the most precious, awesome, baffling and wonderful gift of the Real Presence. But his Body and Blood under the veils of bread and wine are not simply an end in themselves. He intends that we who receive them are to be transformed by them. We too, like Christ, are to become washers of feet. We are to care for the sick, unloved and unlovely. The disciples were about to betray Jesus or run away, but he still washed their feet. We are to follow this example. We cannot all be like Sister Natalie and abandon wealth and privilege to become a Sister in the East End, but we can learn from her example and do similar deeds in our own lives. It is not always easy—Jesus never said it would be—but those Sisters were some of the happiest, most contented, jolly people I have ever known. Day by day they had the Real Presence of Christ in their Eucharist; and, with this precious gift, they understood that they were rich indeed.

1 4

Good Friday

Bishop Fulton Sheen, the famous 1950s and 60s American Roman Catholic preacher and televangelist, once observed that all men and women are born to *live*. Jesus Christ, though, was born to *die*. Today, we remember Jesus' death on the cross at Calvary, just outside the walls of Jerusalem, on Good Friday in AD 33. According to tradition, Jesus was nailed to the cross and it was lifted up at 12 noon, and he died three hours later at 3 o'clock.

A few years ago, Mel Gibson released his film *The Passion of the Christ* about the crucifixion. It created a great stir. One woman left the cinema in tears, saying, "They didn't do that to him, did they?" The answer, of course, is "Yes, they did". Jesus was sentenced to a deliberately painful and degrading execution, the message being that this is what happens to troublemakers. No wonder his friends and disciples were in such a state of shock. Death by crucifixion was a common form of execution in the Roman Empire, but the difference was that this was not an ordinary man being killed. Jesus, his disciples had come to realize, was the Son of God, come to earth to love us and save us. Here he was, hanging in excruciating pain on the cross, his life slowly ebbing away, mocked by the Jewish leaders and by one of the criminals crucified with him. His mother Mary, St John, and a few other women stood nearby, doing what they could to support Jesus simply by being there alongside him in his last, terrible hours.

But why, you might ask, do we call today 'Good Friday'? It was not a very good day for Jesus. It was a horrible, messy death. Evil seemed to have won, and to have overcome the love of God. Well, the answer is that Good Friday was not good for Jesus, but it is good, in its consequences, for us.

Jesus, we need to remind ourselves, came into the world to share our life—and that life includes bodily death for all of us at the end. He also came to deal with the consequences of the Fall, most specifically, with our sins which separate us from God.

Jesus knew he was going to be killed—we know that from his teaching: "The Son of Man must undergo great suffering, and be rejected by the elders, chief priests, and scribes, and be killed, and on the third day be raised" (Luke 9:22). So, he set off in the spring of AD 33 to go to Jerusalem and freely accept his destiny.

As Christ hung on the cross on Good Friday afternoon, things were happening which were invisible to the human eye. With hindsight, we can see that Jesus Christ came into the world for today. He died on the cross, thinking in some wonderful way of you and me, and of every man, woman, boy and girl, offering his life for us in sacrifice to God the Father. Jesus died that we might be forgiven our sins; so that, if we turn in faith to God the Father and sincerely repent, we will be welcomed home like the prodigal son.

Theology, like clothes, has fashions. For about the past ninety years we have tended to stress the resurrection at the expense of the crucifixion. I guess this may have been in some ways a reaction to the loss of so many lives during the First World War. But, of course, we cannot have the resurrection without the crucifixion. Christ is both suffering servant and also risen Lord. This means that when we commit sins, we are in a sense knocking the nails afresh into his hands or jabbing the crown of thorns down again onto his brow. And yet Jesus accepts it. He bears the burden of all of our sins upon his shoulders. And he does so out of love. Whatever we have done, as Christians we should never despair. Jesus Christ has paid the price. He loved us right up unto the end. God can and will forgive us, and grant us a fresh start, if we turn to him.

At the end of the crucifixion they took the dead body of Jesus Christ down from the cross and let his mother hold it just one last time. Then Joseph of Arimathea and Nicodemus hurriedly placed it in the tomb and sealed the entrance. *And that*, they mistakenly thought in their grief, *was that.*

1 5

Easter

To my mind, the most marvellous church in the world is the Church of the Holy Sepulchre in Jerusalem, built over the site of the Easter story. Calvary—also known as Golgotha—where Jesus was crucified, was a scrappy bit of land to the west of Jerusalem; part of it had once been a stone quarry. It was a rubbish dump and the place of execution.

By the time a church came to be built there, the walls of Jerusalem had been knocked down by the Romans in AD 70, the city had grown, and the new city walls covered a larger area, and so the church was now inside Jerusalem. For those of us used to great European cathedrals, the Church of the Holy Sepulchre appears all higgledy-piggledy, with chapels dotted all over the place on several levels. I first went there late one evening, when it was almost deserted, and I instantly fell in love with the place.

When I went back in the morning, the church was heaving with tourists—Americans clutching cameras and Japanese clad in raincoats. I decided to go exploring to avoid the crowds. I spotted some stone stairs and made my way up to a small chapel with an altar in the middle and a single man kneeling in prayer. I read the sign, which told me that this was the site of the crucifixion, and indeed there was a mark beneath the altar showing where the cross of Jesus is supposed to have stood. "How do they know it was *there?*" I asked myself. Then, it dawned on me: that might not be the exact spot, but somewhere around here—give or take a few yards—Jesus had been crucified.

We are used to images of the crucifixion. We see it depicted in stained-glass windows, in oil paintings and on icons, in the form of statues, sometimes embroidered on altar frontals, and frequently worn on chains around people's necks. But here, the *actual* crucifixion of Jesus took place. I knelt on the floor of the chapel, and suddenly, feeling overcome by it all, I found myself weeping—not at all the reaction I would have predicted—and in rather faltering words I prayed, "Thank you, Jesus, for being crucified for me." It did not seem very adequate, but it was the best I could think of at the time.

Climbing down the stairs to the main part of the church, I found that most of the crowds of tourists had now gone, and so I returned to the centre of the church and what is known as the Rotunda. This is the holy sepulchre or tomb of Jesus Christ. It dawned on me that they had not had to carry Jesus very far: his tomb was quite close to the place of execution. When the church was built on the site, the tomb was preserved. Its shape has varied a little over the centuries. You go through quite a small doorway—you have to duck down—along a short passage of about four feet, and then it opens up into a sort of small cave, in which Jesus' body was laid on a shelf.

I found myself wondering—a bit of a silly question—whether they put him in head first, or feet first? It does not really matter, except that it brings home that this was a real place of burial, and it was a corpse that was hurriedly buried in here. The shelf where the body was laid was covered in the early nineteenth century with white stone, because it was being rubbed away by the fingers of countless pilgrims, and other less scrupulous visitors were cutting bits off with penknives and taking them home. Below the white surface, the edge of the original stone can be seen. It is a sort of ginger colour. That is where the body of Jesus was placed, and from there he rose again in the resurrection.

Now, at risk of perhaps upsetting some of you, I am now going to say something very personal. I regret I am not convinced of the authenticity of the so-called Holy Shroud of Turin, which is supposed to contain an image of the dead body of Christ. There are various reasons for this. Quite simply, I do not think that is how God works: we proceed by faith, not by sight. Secondly—and for me, this is decisive—the New Testament makes it plain that the dead body of Jesus was not wrapped in one long, all-encompassing piece of linen, but in two separate pieces. One piece of linen was wrapped around his head. Another covered him from the neck to the feet. When, on the morning of the resurrection, St John and St Peter got to the tomb and went in, they saw the two pieces of linen lying on the shelf. It was a description they would have repeated many times to people who asked them, and it eventually found its way into St John's Gospel.

The resurrection is a mystery. There was no one there with a camera or a notebook and pencil. All that was left was the shelf and the two pieces of linen. I came across one hypothesis which I think quite possible. When Jesus was resurrected, his body was changed. We know this from his later resurrection appearances. He did not sit up and somehow unwind the linen from around him—it would have been difficult as his arms and hands were inside—but rather, he somehow *passed through* the linen, which—with no body left inside to support it—collapsed in on itself. This was what the disciples found left behind on the shelf when they entered the tomb.

The worst thing that could happen—the crucifixion of the incarnate Son of God—has happened; and yet, the love of God is greater still. God's love was so great that even death could not hold Jesus. As he promised, he rose from the dead on the third day.

The resurrection, I guess, separates the men from the boys, or perhaps the sheep from the goats. Many people are prepared to say pleasant things about Jesus—it costs them very little—but he is seen only as a nice man and a good teacher. Someone once pointed out that many people say "Jesus was"—he is a historical figure—whereas Christian men and women of faith say "Jesus is"—he is a living reality, a part of their daily lives.

If we believe in the resurrection, it strikes me that there are a couple of important consequences for us. The resurrection confirms the identity of Jesus Christ: he really *is* the Son of God. This means we have to take his teaching, his words and deeds in the Gospels, seriously. We cannot cherry-pick, or say that a bit does not apply to us, or that Jesus would have done it differently and been more in tune with the spirit of our age had he lived later. Christianity is about freely giving our hearts to Jesus, and allowing him to possess them, and that means allowing ourselves to be guided by him.

Secondly, the resurrection speaks to us of Christ's ultimate victory over sin, evil and death. Death itself could not hold Jesus. The same applies to all who love and trust him. We too shall enjoy a resurrection like his. Our journey begins now, in this life, on planet earth.

Going into the tomb and trying to imagine the unimaginable—the resurrection—was a very moving and powerful experience. It was also a surprisingly peaceful one. Like many generations of pilgrims before me, I followed the ancient tradition and bought my own shroud from a shop just outside the church, and briefly laid it on the shelf in the tomb of Christ. It now sits in a box in my desk, ready to be used when the time comes, a little, final symbol of my personal faith and trust in the Easter story and its eternal significance.

If we sought a sentence to sum up the message of the resurrection, it is that *Jesus, the Prince of Peace, is also Jesus, the Lord of Life*. May I wish you all a very happy and blessed Easter.

1 6

The Ascension

The ascension of Jesus Christ is forever associated in my mind with camel fleas. When I visited Jerusalem, I walked across a valley and made my way up a steep hill to the Chapel of the Ascension on the top of the Mount of Olives. On the way, I had to squeeze past some camels who were blocking my way. They were nasty, smelly, bad-tempered animals, and a little later I found I had acquired lots of flea bites. A day to remember.

My goal, at the top of the Mount of Olives, was a little chapel built by the Crusaders on the spot from where Jesus is said to have ascended back to heaven forty days after the resurrection. My thoughts here were similar to those in Nazareth or Bethlehem. In the Church of the Annunciation in Nazareth I was struck by the thought, "This is where it all began." At Bethlehem, in the so-called stable under the altar of the Church of the Nativity I thought "Here the Son of God was born." Standing on top of the Mount of Olives I thought "Here the story ends, for from here he went back to heaven."

It is the unique claim of Christianity to have been founded not by a prophet, nor by a good man, nor by a guru, but by the Son of God come to earth. We have heard the story so often that our ears have become used to it and our sense of wonder has worn thin: God, whom we cannot see, sent his only Son to earth to share our ordinary human life. Jesus Christ is perfect God and perfect man. He came to reveal divine truth to us, to die upon the cross in sacrifice for our sins, and to rise from the dead three days later. For thirty-three years, God's only Son trod the soil of Palestine, where all could see him, and at the end he returned to heaven.

We no more understand how God brought about the ascension than we understand how he brought about the incarnation or the resurrection; but then, it really is none of our business. God reveals to us what he wants us to understand, and what we do not understand, we must accept in faith. If we do not understand how the ascension happened, we do grasp its meaning. When Jesus was born of the Virgin Mary at Bethlehem, he took his humanity from Mary and his divinity from God, his heavenly Father: thus he was both perfectly human and also perfectly divine.

But when he ascended back to heaven thirty-three years later, he took with him something he did not bring with him to earth: his human body and all his experiences during his lifetime.

When we pray, we address a God who now knows from the inside, as it were, what it is like to be human: to be loved and valued by mother, stepfather and friends, to feel the warmth of the sun and the cold of the winter, to be healthy and to be sick, to mourn the death of a stepfather and of a dear friend, Lazarus, to be hated and reviled by enemies, to be sinned against, lied about, betrayed, killed. With the exception of personal sin, for he never sinned, Jesus Christ knows exactly what we go through day by day. The Creator shared the life of the created. In the Epistle to the Hebrews this great truth is presented to us as a source of comfort and encouragement in the life of prayer and faith:

> Since, then, we have a great high priest who has passed through the heavens, Jesus, the Son of God, let us hold fast to our confession. For we do not have a high priest who is unable to sympathize with us in our weaknesses, but we have one who in every respect has been tested as we are, yet without sin. Let us therefore approach the throne of grace with boldness, so that we may receive mercy and find grace to help in time of need.
>
> *Hebrews 4:14–16*

Christianity is a historical religion. This means that it is based upon a concrete happening in the past, the life of Jesus Christ in the first century. But it is more than just that. In his teachings, Jesus taught us things that are true for all eternity. The effects of his life, death and resurrection reach forward into all the centuries that our world will exist and beyond them. The surprising thing about the ascension is that the disciples were not sad when Jesus returned to heaven. You would have expected them to be heartbroken—after all, they had only just got him back from the dead in the resurrection—but not a bit of it. St Luke tells us '[They] returned to Jerusalem with great joy; and they were continually in the temple blessing God' (Luke 24:52–53). Jesus, you see, had promised that he would not leave them desolate, but would send the Comforter, the Holy Spirit, to be with them: "And see, I am sending upon you what my Father promised; so stay here in the city until you have been clothed with power from on high" (Luke 24:49). What does this mean? Well, come back at Pentecost and find out.

1 7

Pentecost

When we went on pilgrimage recently, I took a book to read on the plane. It is called *The Enthusiast*, and it is about a man called the Revd Joseph Leycester Lyne, or Father Ignatius, Abbot of Llanthony Abbey in Wales.

Joseph was born in 1837, the son of a prosperous City of London merchant. As a young man, he visited Devonport and was very impressed by the newly founded Anglican religious sisterhood there. It was a time when several religious communities were being established for women in the Church of England, and Joseph had the idea of starting one for men following the Rule of Saint Benedict. It became his life's work, and he changed his name to Ignatius.

Unfortunately, although Ignatius possessed boundless enthusiasm and a charismatic personality, he also had the unfortunate knack of rubbing people up the wrong way and was rather lacking in judgement and tact. He was ordained as a deacon, but managed to upset so many bishops, including the Archbishop of Canterbury, that no one was prepared to ordain him to the priesthood. He would, for example, visit country clergy with a few of his monks, ostensibly just for a few days, and end up staying for several months, much to the chagrin of the vicar's family and parishioners.

In the end, Ignatius established a monastery at Llanthony in South Wales. Ignatius was a gifted preacher and would conduct preaching missions across the country. His motto was 'Jesus Only', and he delivered wonderful sermons about putting Jesus first in our lives. Whenever Ignatius preached, there was standing room only, and the crowds spilled out into the streets. He could melt the hearts of rough dockyard workers, as well as of professional men and gentry. The collections taken at these services paid for the monastery.

Unfortunately, Ignatius kept control of the money himself, and would not trust any of the other monks to help. I think he put it in an old sock, and every time they needed to pay for something, he would dip into the sock. When funds became low, he would go and carry out another preaching mission. As well as controlling the money, he also refused to delegate any other tasks to anyone else.

Ignatius' other problem was that he was a terrible judge of character. He was fleeced left, right and centre by the builders, who built him a shoddy chapel and charged him the earth. As far as recruiting monks went, Ignatius naively believed everything people told him about themselves: they were Christians, seeking to follow 'Jesus Only', he would have said to himself, so why did he need to check up on them? Ignatius did not have much notion of testing the spirits, to use New Testament language. This meant that if you told him a sob-story, he would admit you as a postulant monk. Men with genuine vocations found themselves living alongside those with none, or worse. On one occasion when Ignatius was away conducting a mission, the Police raided the monastery and arrested a postulant, who turned out to be a criminal on the run. On another occasion, Ignatius admitted a teenage boy to the monastery who claimed that God wanted him to be a monk. In fact, the boy was going through a teenage religious phase, and also rebelling against his father, who sued Ignatius in the courts to get his son back. On another occasion, Ignatius tried hard for several months to persuade a novice having doubts about his vocation to stay. In the end, the man left, became a milkman, married and had a large family.

Still, Ignatius was a lovable man, and could speak wonderfully about Jesus. He died in 1908. Crowds attended his funeral, and he was buried in front of the altar in the abbey chapel. Sadly, within three years, his monastery had closed, principally because of his silly way of running it. The jerry-built chapel cracked; the weeds found their way in; and the whole thing eventually collapsed.

You may say, "Well, this is all very interesting, but what has it got to do with Pentecost?" One of Ignatius' biographers wrote that, to quote Jesus' words, Ignatius loved the Lord his God with all his heart, with all his soul, and with all his strength. And yet, if you are familiar with that passage from St Mark, you will have spotted that there is something missing. Jesus also said that we must love the Lord our God with all our *mind*. Ignatius did not use his mind to serve God. He was carried away by enthusiasm, emotionalism, perhaps by romanticism, and certainly, to be fair, by generosity of heart and spirit. But mind: no.

That is where the Holy Spirit fits in. When we speak of the mind, we mean a bit more than merely the brain, the organ inside our skull. We are thinking of things such as character, thoughtfulness, wisdom, experience and insight, all of which make us the men and women we are.

We might further reflect on the sort of things that influence our minds. In no particular order, I would suggest: God's grace in all its forms, baptism, holy communion, prayer and the life of faith, reading the Bible, public worship, the example of the lives of the saints, confession and absolution, being forgiven and learning to forgive others, giving and receiving love, forbearance, receiving from the generosity of others and learning to be generous ourselves, managing not to harbour grudges, trying to control our thoughts and tongues, taking the wider view of things, thinking of others.

These are all ways—there are, of course, many more—in which the Holy Spirit is constantly at work in us, guiding and shaping our minds. His aim, in all things, is to draw us closer to the mind of Christ. Ignatius wasn't so wrong in his motto, 'Jesus Only'. To hear some people preach or write about Pentecost, one might be forgiven for thinking that the Holy Spirit is all about escapism—running away from the world in which we are placed. I suggest that actually the Holy Spirit is all about trying to make some sense of the world in which we are placed, coping with the difficult and painful bits, and striving to do a little good whilst we are on earth.

Returning to the list of things that influence our minds which I mentioned above, how do we expect the Holy Spirit to help us, if not through such means? Some people seem to expect to find the Holy Spirit only in what we might call the dramatic. Well, the Holy Spirit certainly can be dramatic, at the times and in the circumstances of his own choice; but I suggest he is more often to be encountered in the immediate and obvious.

There is another important point about the Holy Spirit. I do not know if you have ever been to a swimming pool and watched a mother or father encouraging their child to swim a width. When the width has been swum, often they will say, "That was really good. Next time, you will do even better and swim a length."

The Holy Spirit is an encourager, and sometimes he encourages us to step outside our comfort zone and do things that feel a bit strange. Think of St Augustine, trudging nervously across Europe to re-establish Christianity in England; think of the monks who built our great abbeys and cathedrals, to express their praise of God in stone; think of Mother Teresa and her wonderful work in Calcutta; think of an artist or a doctor, of a writer or a parent. All in their own ways are inspired by the Holy Spirit to take a little step in faith, and then another one after that. As a small boy, I used to hate blood, but some of my richest experiences as a priest have been with the sick and dying. I would never have expected that. Nor did I ever expect to become a chaplain to St John Ambulance: God has a sense of humour.

God has a plan and a purpose for each of us during our lives on earth. The Holy Spirit is busy, nurturing us throughout, so that we may play our part in it, whether we are aware of it or not.

I want to end with poor old Father Ignatius, Abbot of Llanthony. A bit of a silly man, but gifted in many ways, too. As I said, his abbey soon crumbled away and was forgotten. But not quite. Twenty-five years after Ignatius' death, some people decided to erect a stone cross at Llanthony in his memory. They wondered if anyone would come to its dedication. To their amazement, from across the Valleys and from further afield, people arrived in their hundreds, by train, bus, car, bicycle and on foot. They were all people whose lives, in some way, had been touched by Ignatius. Even the reluctant novice, who became a milkman, retained a great affection for Ignatius all his life and wrote a little book about him.

The point? Well, the Holy Spirit takes our poor efforts and uses them in God's service. Sometimes, I find myself walking back down a garden path after a pastoral visit and thinking, "Well Lord, that didn't go too well, did it?" I offer it all up, and sometimes I hear on the grapevine that my visit had more of an impact than I expected. I find myself humbled and yet cheered. This is all the work of the Holy Spirit. God rejects nothing of what we offer him but takes it and weaves it into his own plan and purpose. Ignatius might have been carried away by his own enthusiasm, a bit eccentric and gullible, but he was also full of love. As all the people who turned up to the dedication of his memorial cross showed, the Holy Spirit had used his love to reach out and touch hundreds of lives for the good.

One of the marks of the Holy Spirit is that he always directs attention away from himself and towards the Son of God. Perhaps then, on this Pentecost Sunday, we could do a lot worse than ponder Ignatius' motto, and make it our own: *Jesus Only.*

Trinity Sunday

Useful visual aid: three and a half bottles of the same wine

When I was a little boy in Sunday school, I once overheard one of the Sunday school teachers saying to another teacher, "Oh, the doctrine of the Holy Trinity is *very hard* to understand." This negative remark took root in my young head, and for some while, whenever the Holy Trinity was mentioned in church, I switched off, thinking that this was too hard for me.

Everything changed some years afterwards when, as an undergraduate, I found myself studying the doctrine of the Holy Trinity. I found myself captivated, excited and moved. It became clear to me that the doctrine of the Holy Trinity is the *key* doctrine of Christianity, upon which everything else rests. When I was ordained a priest in 1989, I chose for my first Mass to celebrate a Eucharist of the Holy Trinity in recognition of its importance.

We need to understand from the outset that the Holy Trinity is a mystery which God has revealed to us. We sometimes talk of the 'otherness' of God: he is completely different from us human beings. Rightly has it been suggested that a newly born baby knows as much of the world and its ways as a man or woman knows about God.

But—and it is a big *but*—that is not the whole picture. The exciting truth is that men and women *may* know something about God, because God has chosen to reveal himself to us. Supremely, he has chosen to do so through his Son, our Lord Jesus Christ.

We must remind ourselves that Jesus' first followers were all Jewish. One of the principal characteristics of the Jews was that they were fiercely monotheistic—they taught that there is only one God—as opposed to the peoples of surrounding lands who were polytheistic and worshipped a great assortment of deities. For these Jewish disciples of Christ, the nature of the coming of Jesus Christ posed a huge intellectual challenge. They had all expected the Messiah to be a sort of Davidic warrior-prince, a man uniquely inspired and used by God, but still only a man. It gradually became clear to the disciples and first generation of Christians that Jesus was far more than this. He was a man like the rest of us, but he was also divine, the Son of God come to earth. He even told us to refer to God his Father as 'Abba', which means something like 'Dad' or 'Papa'.

Then, there was the experience of the Holy Spirit (sometimes also known as the Holy Ghost) at Pentecost, which happened just as Jesus had said it would. How were the first Christians to understand the wonderful, new outpouring of the Holy Spirit upon the fledgling Christian Church?

The first generations of Christians had to grapple with this challenge, and they had to evolve new words and concepts in order to do so. What the Church eventually came to see was that God—as the Jews were keen to stress—is One: there is only One God, there are not three Gods. And yet, we are privileged to know God in three ways, or, as they put it, as three 'Persons': God the Father, the source and creator of everything there is; God the Son, our Lord Jesus Christ, who has always existed, who became incarnate in the womb of the Blessed Virgin Mary, was born, lived on earth, was crucified and resurrected, and returned to heaven at the ascension; and God the Holy Spirit, the Paraclete or Comforter, who makes things holy and is constantly at work in the world. The three 'Persons' are quite distinct from each other and are not to be confused, and yet they all share the same 'essence' or 'substance', which is to say they are all God. Whoever partakes of one person partakes of all three. To take one scriptural example, we can see all three Persons of the Holy Trinity in the story of the annunciation: the Angel Gabriel brings Mary a message from God the Father; Jesus Christ becomes incarnate in her womb; and this is all brought about by the overshadowing of the Holy Spirit. Building upon the earlier work of the Council of Nicaea in AD 325, the doctrine of the Holy Trinity was formally defined by the Council of Constantinople in AD 381.

One of the most engaging accounts of the doctrine of the Holy Trinity I have come across is in Graham Greene's 1982 novel, *Monsignor Quixote*.

Set in Spain shortly after the death of General Franco, while Europe was still divided by the Iron Curtain and the Cold War, the book is about Father Quixote, Roman Catholic parish priest of the small and obscure country parish of El Toboso, who believes that he is a descendant of Cervantes' fictional character, Don Quixote.

One day, Father Quixote helps an Italian bishop from the Vatican whose car has broken down. Some weeks later Father Quixote is surprised to discover that his reward for helping the bishop is his appointment as a *monsignor*. A monsignor is an official in the papal household and is an honour, akin to receiving a medal in the Queen's birthday honours. Father Quixote sets off on a little holiday and to buy the new robes of a monsignor, accompanied by his friend Sancho, a former seminarian and now a Marxist. Graham Greene's novel is about the adventures the two men enjoy on their journey.

At one point, Father Quixote and Sancho stop for a picnic and unpack the copious repast packed for them by Father Quixote's housekeeper, Teresa. The wine flows, and Sancho asks his friend "Can you explain the Trinity to me? It was more than they could do at Salamanca."

Father Quixote says he can try, and, rummaging around in the picnic basket produces two and a half bottles of the local wine which Teresa has packed. "Two bottles," he says, "equal in size. The wine they contained was of the same substance, and it was born at the same time. There you have God the Father and God the Son and there, in the half bottle you have God the Holy Ghost. Same substance. Same birth. They're inseparable. Whoever partakes of one partakes of all three."

After a while Sancho realizes that Father Quixote is quietly weeping. He asks him what on earth is the matter. Between his tears, Father Quixote says he is guilty of heresy; he has sinned, and he is perhaps not worthy to be a priest. What has he done? "I have given wrong instruction," he explains. "The Holy Ghost is equal in all respects to the Father and the Son, and I have represented him by this half bottle."[11]

Sancho—I imagine him smiling—tells Father Quixote not to worry; the matter is easily put right. They should simply ignore the half bottle of wine—and, going to the car, he produces a third, full bottle of wine, to represent the Holy Spirit.

I said at the start that I found the doctrine of the Holy Trinity captivating, exciting and moving. Why? God is completely 'other' to men and women. I am amazed—bowled over—by the realization that God has chosen to reveal himself to us, and supremely to do so through the incarnation of his only Son, Jesus Christ our Lord.

Think how much God must love us.

Reservation of the Blessed Sacrament

A sermon for Corpus Christi

The first generations of Christians valued Holy Communion very highly. To begin with, there were no special church buildings: Christians met to celebrate the Eucharist in their houses, sometimes in great secrecy when the Church was being persecuted by the Roman Empire. Many Christians, facing the possibility of death by martyrdom, desired to receive their Lord in Holy Communion daily. This was the origin of reservation of the Blessed Sacrament: it is a Christian devotional custom which would have been familiar to the grandchildren of some of the people who knew Jesus.

In addition to receiving Holy Communion during the Eucharist, the early Christians were often given some of the sacramental body of Christ to take away with them. They would 'reserve' the sacrament at home, pray quietly each day and then consume some of the sacrament from the previous Sunday. From the very earliest days, it was seen as important to treat the reserved sacrament with great care and reverence. Several sermons survive from this period in which weak-willed Christians were castigated for going to the public games with the Blessed Sacrament still in their pockets.

The clergy, too, began to reserve the sacrament in their houses in order that they might administer Holy Communion in a hurry to the sick and dying. After the conversion of the Emperor Constantine to Christianity in AD 315, special buildings for Christian worship—churches—began to be built around the Roman Empire. The ending of the persecution meant that it was possible to celebrate the Eucharist openly and with greater frequency. The clergy now began to reserve the sacrament in their new churches, and the old custom of giving the congregation enough sacrament to take home on Sunday to last them for a week slowly faded away.

Reservation of the sacrament might thus be described as a devotional movement generated from the bottom up: it was not imposed from above by the bishops, but it grew out of the deep desire of the first generations of persecuted Christians to receive their Lord in Holy Communion on a daily basis. Reservation of the sacrament in churches received a boost from the ecumenical Council of Nicaea in AD 325 which, as well as giving us the Nicene Creed, also required all Christians to be given Holy Communion on their deathbeds as *viaticum* or food for the journey.

In 1054, the Christian Church was unfortunately split by the Great Schism into what became known as the Roman Catholic Church in Western Europe, and as the Orthodox Church in Eastern Europe. Both Churches practised reservation of the sacrament. In Roman Catholic churches, reservation was continuous; whereas in Orthodox churches, reservation was carried out only at certain times of the year, for example during Great Lent.

Initially, reservation of the sacrament was undertaken very simply in both the Roman Catholic and Orthodox Churches. However, from the thirteenth century, starting in Germany and the Low Countries and slowly spreading across the Roman Catholic Church in Western Europe, the reserved sacrament began to be used by Christians as an aid to prayer and focus of devotion. Like reservation itself, this was a spiritual movement generated from the bottom up, which grew out of the desire of medieval Christians to draw ever closer to Jesus Christ in his sacramental presence. It was formally acknowledged by the creation of the feast of Corpus Christi in 1264.

During the English Reformation in the sixteenth century, temporary reservation of the sacrament for the communion of the sick and dying was initially enjoined in the first *Book of Common Prayer* of 1549. Subsequent *Prayer Books* made no provision for reservation, and by the second half of the sixteenth century the practice had largely died out. In Scotland, however, the Scottish Episcopal Church came to appreciate the value of reservation of the sacrament for communion of the sick and dying, and from the eighteenth century the sacrament was reserved in Scottish Episcopalian churches. In the nineteenth century, the Oxford

Movement in the Church of England led to a greater appreciation of the Eucharist, as well as higher pastoral expectations and better care— including sacramental care—of the sick. The sacrament once more began to be reserved in churches in England and across the worldwide Anglican Communion. In 1911 and 1929, the bishops of the Church of England agreed upon regulations for the reservation of the sacrament. Today, the sacrament is reserved in the Archbishop of Canterbury's chapel at Lambeth Palace, in every English cathedral, in most hospital chapels, and in a great many parish churches across the provinces of Canterbury and York.

Reservation of the sacrament is a very great help to pastoral work. In all parishes it is sometimes necessary to administer Holy Communion in a hurry. Someone may suddenly be taken ill, or suffer an accident, and may wish to receive Holy Communion. It is not always possible to celebrate the Eucharist: the priest may have to administer Holy Communion to someone at the scene of a motor accident, in the pouring rain.

I know from experience that many sick and housebound parishioners greatly value receiving Holy Communion at home. There are also occasions when pastoral necessity renders it appropriate to give Holy Communion from the reserved sacrament to people who are physically well but otherwise in need. I can think of one of my parishioners who suffered a devastating and life-altering shock. I took him to church, where we prayed quietly together before the altar, and at the end I gave him Holy Communion from the reserved sacrament.

There are three ways of reserving the sacrament in the Church of England. The *aumbry* is a lockable cupboard, set into a wall, into which the sacrament is placed. The *tabernacle* is a small cupboard for the sacrament, usually affixed to the back of an altar, but sometimes freestanding. The hanging *pyx* is a container for the sacrament suspended from chains before the high altar. It is usual to hang a lamp inside a white or red glass nearby, as a sign that the sacrament is reserved there.

One prayer with which we are all familiar is the *Agnus Dei*:

> *O Lamb of God, that takest away the sins of the world, have mercy on us.*
> *O Lamb of God, that takest away the sins of the world, have mercy on us.*
> *O Lamb of God, that takest away the sins of the world, grant us thy peace.*

These words have been a part of the Eucharist, between the consecration
and communion, since at least the seventh century AD. They are an act
of adoration of Jesus Christ in his sacramental presence. Christians
have long been accustomed to treat the sacrament not just with care, but
also with love and devotion. St Francis of Assisi, among many others,
encouraged Christians to love Jesus Christ in his holy sacrament.

This love of Christ's sacramental presence ties in with reservation.
One of the unlooked-for gifts of God is the special atmosphere of
stillness and peace that builds up in the part of the church wherever the
sacrament is reserved. I remember noticing this stillness as a boy, long
before I understood about the real presence. In many cathedrals and large
churches, the chapel containing the aumbry or tabernacle is set aside for
private prayer. Many Christians enjoy simply popping in to the part of
their church where the sacrament is reserved, to spend a few minutes in
quiet prayer, soaking up the peaceful atmosphere.

A number of parish churches also have services in connection with
the Blessed Sacrament, such as Devotions or Benediction, during
which hymns, prayers and Bible readings are said and sung before the
reserved sacrament, which becomes a focus of prayer and worship. One
custom from between the wars which might helpfully be revived is that
of Christians gathering before the aumbry or tabernacle on Saturday,
perhaps after Evensong, to say prayers to prepare themselves to receive
Holy Communion on Sunday.

The Church of England's *Revised Common Lectionary* makes provision
for the 'Thanksgiving for Holy Communion', more commonly known as
Corpus Christi, on the first available Thursday after Trinity Sunday. On
Maundy Thursday we remember Christ instituting the Eucharist at the
Last Supper; but our joy is overshadowed by his betrayal at Gethsemane
and impending crucifixion the next day on Good Friday. On Corpus
Christi, by contrast, these sombre elements are absent; and we offer Jesus
Christ our joyful adoration of his precious gift to us of his body and blood
in the Blessed Sacrament.

I have been ordained a priest for over thirty years. During that time, I
have worked in some very diverse parishes in the dioceses of Portsmouth,
Leicester and Chelmsford. The sacrament was reserved in all the parish
churches, and this proved to be a very great boon. Week by week, I have

taken the reserved sacrament to housebound parishioners, to those who are ill or recovering after surgery. A few times each year, the telephone has rung, and I have found myself hurrying to a house or hospital to administer the sacrament to a dying Christian. Sometimes they have died, and sometimes they have recovered. It is all a most marvellous ministry, and I am grateful to God for calling me to it.

At the same time, being a priest can be tough and demanding. I have been grateful on many occasions for the atmosphere of peace and stillness that has built up around the reserved sacrament. After some particularly difficult pastoral experience, or when a long and demanding day has left me feeling weary, I have frequently found myself flopping down at the communion rail, offering it all up to the Lord Jesus and for a few minutes seeking solace and renewed strength in his sacramental presence. When it has been hard to find the right words with which to pray, a short time spent by the aumbry or tabernacle has somehow sorted it all out. The right words form themselves in one's mind, the solution to a nagging problem is revealed, the way forward becomes clear, and one finds that one receives strength to get up and carry on.

Nor should the influence of the little white or red lamp burning before the reserved sacrament be underestimated. Many times during the course of a week, one will enter the parish church to do or to fetch something. There, in the distance, the lamp flickers, the little flame dancing in joy, as it were, at the sacramental presence of the Lord Jesus Christ. The lamp reminds us that, beyond that which is visible and temporal, lies that which is unseen and eternal. It speaks to us of the quiet, gentle, abiding love of God for all his children. Whatever we do or say, whatever sins we commit, or daft ideas we get into our heads, the lamp still flickers, and Jesus Christ is still present, offering limitless love, forgiveness and grace to all who believe in him. Rushing into church in search of a service paper or book, one catches a glimpse of the little lamp burning before the sacrament. In the midst of our busyness, it bids us to remember the things of God, and it urges us to do just a little bit more out of love for Jesus Christ that day.

2 0

Bible Sunday

I have spent years studying the Bible, but I have to confess that the best sermon I ever heard preached about the Bible was at a children's service in Manchester. The preacher produced a rucksack. "We Christians are going on a journey through life to God," he told the children. "This is my rucksack. It contains lots of things I take when I go walking. The Bible is just like this. It contains lots of things to help us on our journey to God. Shall we see what's inside?"

First he produced a map. "This map shows me where I'm going when I walk. The Bible shows us the way to God."

Then he drew out a compass. "When I walk the wrong way, the compass points me back in the right direction. If I go the wrong way as a Christian, the Bible points me back to the path to God."

Next, he produced a torch. "Sometimes it can get dark when I am out walking. That can be a bit frightening. The torch guides me through the dark and reassures me I'll get home in one piece. Sometimes it is difficult being a Christian. The Bible guides me when I'm anxious and reassures me I'll be all right."

Lastly he withdrew his packed lunch. "I get very hungry when I'm out walking, so I need some food. The Bible also feeds me and helps me grow as a Christian."

That sermon was preached over thirty years ago, and it has stuck in my head ever since. The preacher managed to say some very profound things about the Bible in a very simple way, which could be grasped by small children and also by adults.

Why is the Bible—also sometimes known as Holy Scripture—so significant for us Christians? Well, for a start it is great literature. It is a good read; it contains history, drama, poetry, law, songs, prayers and teaching. There are passages which have inspired saints to do wonderful feats for God. There are passages to bring comfort in times of sorrow. There are some very funny bits. Anyone who says the Bible is boring clearly has not read it very closely.

But there is a far more important reason why we esteem the Bible. We believe that God the Holy Spirit inspired the human authors of the texts that make up the Old and New Testaments. The writers of the various parts of the Bible made use of their own intellectual faculties, literary and editorial skills, but God acted in them and through them. They consigned to writing whatever God wanted written, and no more. That is why we refer to the Bible as the word of the Lord. I suppose we might say there were many different writers, but one divine author.

At this point I ought to interject that the Bible, being a collection of works over many centuries, contains bits that are easy to understand and bits that are puzzling. You will recall that St Peter did not always find St Paul's letters very easy. There are also a few passages which seem contradictory. It is important that we use our brains when we read the Bible, and avoid the dangers of a narrow, unreflective fundamentalism. That is where the Christian Church comes in. The Bible is the Church's book. It is meant to be read in the context of the community of the faithful. One of the tasks of the Church is to interpret the Bible to each generation of Christians. The Church of England teaches that the Bible contains all things necessary to salvation, so that unless something can be read in the Bible or proved from it, it may not be required of anyone as an article of faith. You may hold an idea that cannot be directly proved from the Bible as a pious opinion, but that is all. It is important that our understanding of this teaching about the Bible is appropriately nuanced—there are a number of Christian doctrines which are found *in embryo* in the Bible, which later generations have had to tease out, such as the nature of the Holy Trinity or the dual nature of Christ—but I have long thought this teaching about the Bible to be a sensible antidote to some of the weird ideas which have done the rounds in all generations.

It is also worth reminding ourselves that although the Bible dates from a certain period of history, it contains teachings which are eternal. It is authored by God, after all. There are many parts of the Bible which our modern society finds difficult. Think, for instance, of the Old Testament's teaching about the sanctity of life in the womb before birth, or Christ's teaching about marriage, or the strong emphasis running through both the Old and New Testaments about the dignity of each and every human being and the sin of exploiting the weak. "The Church needs to come up to date," people sometimes say. But they have fundamentally misunderstood Christianity. What matters is not "being up to date", but conforming ourselves with, and sharing in, that which is eternal; that, indeed, to which the Bible bears witness.

I draw to a close with a wonderful collect for the second Sunday in Advent from the 1662 *Prayer Book,* which I am sure is familiar to you: 'Blessed Lord, who caused all holy Scriptures to be written for our learning: help us so to hear them, to read, mark, learn and inwardly digest them, that, through patience, and the comfort of your holy word, we may embrace and for ever hold fast the hope of everlasting life, which you have given us in our Saviour, Jesus Christ.'

Read, mark, learn, and inwardly digest. We are expected to read the Bible, to think about it, and to absorb it into our daily lives. We come to church on Sundays, amongst other reasons, to hear the Bible read out. But more than that, we should try to read the Bible at home on weekdays too. Now, I know we are all busy people, and it is not easy to fit in time for reading the Bible. But it does not take long just to read a few verses: as long as it takes to drink a cup of tea. Many people find Bible notes helpful. There are several different sorts. You read a little passage each day and then there is a page telling you all about it. I commend the idea to you.

I end, as I began, with a reminder that for Christians, the Bible is our map, our compass, our torch, and our food. Not a luxury, but a necessity on our journey through life to God.

Baptism: Joined to Christ

Regenerate and grafted into the body of Christ's Church

I thought the other day of my grandfather, who was what I would call a 'plantsman' rather than a gardener, because he was not remotely interested in creating a beautifully laid out garden, but who enjoyed a deep and lifelong fascination with botany and plants of all shapes and sizes. He had a large, nineteenth-century house in London, with a higgledy-piggledy garden at the back. He created three large raised flowerbeds, edged with concrete. Large and small terracotta flowerpots, cloches and cold frames were dotted about the place, and at the far end there were two Heath-Robinson greenhouses of his own devising. In this garden, my grandfather pottered for well over thirty years. As I say, he was not particularly interested in creating a garden as such, but he delighted in cultivating awkward plants and seeds that were difficult to grow, or were perhaps from other parts of the world and did not much care for the English climate. My grandfather was especially interested in using cuttings.

Sometimes he would *graft* a cutting onto another plant. Grafting is often employed with roses and vines, but it can also be used with some other plants. You get a sharp knife and cut the end of your cutting into a long, pointed arrowhead shape. You then make a V-shaped incision into the growing plant onto which you wish to graft the cutting. You ease the cutting into the incision and bind it up. With luck, it will take, and will become part of the original plant. The two pieces will grow together, and the life flows up from the roots into the bit you have grafted on.

Jesus' words to Nicodemus, "No one can enter the kingdom of God without being born of water and Spirit" (John 3:5) have traditionally been thought to be about baptism. When Archbishop Thomas Cranmer was writing the *Book of Common Prayer*, he wondered how he might explain what baptism meant to largely rural and agricultural congregations. It occurred to the archbishop—perhaps he had been thinking of the parable of the vine—that baptism is rather like grafting a cutting onto a plant.

When we are baptized, we are 'grafted' onto the Easter story and onto the saving work of Christ. The death of Jesus on the cross on Good Friday and his glorious resurrection from the dead three days later on Easter Day is no longer just something that happened a long time ago. Just as the cutting is given life and fed by the roots of the plant onto which it is grafted, so we are given eternal life and fed by Jesus Christ, to whom we are joined by baptism.

There is a very old custom you sometimes see at funeral services. The priest will walk around the coffin sprinkling it with a little holy water. This is a reminder that the person who died was baptized and thus joined to Jesus Christ. Their body has died, just as Jesus once died upon the cross, but because they are joined to Christ, they will be raised up by God in a resurrection, just like Jesus.

Baptism is quite literally the foundation of everything in the Christian life. We all have many big and important days in our lives, but the day we are baptized is the most important day we can ever have, because it grafts us onto Easter. Baptism bears fruit in our lives in this world, and also in the life of the world to come.

Marriage

Preached at the wedding of my friends Nicolas and Kirsty

It is a truth, universally acknowledged, that a wedding and an alcoholic booze-up go together. It was so in the first century AD when Our Lord Jesus Christ attended a wedding in the village of Cana. The couple getting married were very poor. They had done their best, but in those days wedding feasts lasted for three days, and everyone had come from the surrounding villages in search of a free meal and drink. Before long, the wine ran out. You can imagine the embarrassment of bride and groom. Prompted by his mother Mary, Christ performed his first miracle. He turned water into wine, and there was enough for everyone.

The Church has always thought that if the first miracle Christ performed—the first thing he did to show that he was the Son of God—was at a wedding, then, in God's eyes weddings and marriage are very important.

And more. This story contains a note of humour, for when the steward tasted the water turned into wine, he came up to the groom and said (my translation): "You're a funny one! Most people serve the good wine first, and then, when everyone has had a few drinks and is feeling a bit squiffy, they bring out the plonk; but you've done it the other way round. You've served the cheap wine first, and saved the good wine until now!"

Of course, we groan as we read this, for we realize that all the poor man has been able to afford is cheap, thin wine, and not much of it. Christ, though, has turned the water into excellent wine, of the best vintage. This good wine represents all the good things that God wishes to give his children through marriage and married life.

Nicolas and Kirsty: God has called you to marry each other. It is your *vocation*, the way of life he wants you to lead on earth, in which you are to grow and to serve him. And in this vocation, he wishes to give you much good wine, many wonderful and enriching things.

In a few minutes you, Nicolas, will place a wedding ring on Kirsty's finger. That ring tells us a lot about marriage. (1) It is made of gold, the most precious thing on earth. (2) It is a circle, a perfect shape. (3) The goldsmith has fashioned it in one piece, so there is no join, no beginning and no end.

Nicolas and Kirsty: in each other's eyes you are the most precious thing in the world. God has called you and entrusted you to each other.

In your married life together, you will perfect and shape one another: you will draw out the good in each other and walk hand in hand on your pilgrimage through life to God.

Your marriage vows will be consecrated by God. They are permanent and irrevocable, and will be dissolved only by death, no beginning and no end. You came to this church a bachelor and a spinster: you will leave it a married couple, with 'Married to Nicolas' and 'Married to Kirsty' stamped upon your souls.

Knowing me, as you do, it would not be a proper sermon if I did not mention Archbishop Cosmo Gordon Lang. Archbishop Lang once wrote that no couple, on their wedding day, can pledge that their married life together will all be plain sailing: life, as we know, is not like that. But what they can pledge is that their married life together will be noble.

He went on to ask the question: how can they make their married life noble? The answer is very simple: by consciously, deliberately, sharing it with Jesus Christ, and allowing him to be their guide.

Well, you have got off to a good start, and furnished the rest of us with a fine example, by setting your wedding within a Nuptial Mass. For in a few minutes, you will both kneel before the altar of God, and there you will together receive Jesus Christ in his sacramental presence in Holy Communion. And, for a few seconds, we shall see a most powerful image: for there will be Nicolas and Kirsty, and Jesus Christ coming to both of you in your Communion. Let his love flow in, and guide and direct your love.

When I got up this morning, I thought "Oh good, it's the day of Nicolas and Kirsty's wedding." Everyone here today is excited and pleased for you. But our excitement, our love, is as nothing compared with the excitement and love of God, who has always planned that you will meet and marry. He looks down from heaven, and today, quite literally, sends his blessing upon you. Share your married life and your home with him. And be assured that God, who has called you, will never forget you.

The last word today must go not to a priest, but to a poet. Some words by Samuel Taylor Coleridge:

> And in Life's noisiest hour,
> There whispers still the ceaseless love of Thee,
> The heart's self-solace and soliloquy.
> You mould my Hopes, you fashion me within;
> And to the leading Love-throb in the Heart
> Thro' all my Being, thro' all my pulses beat;
> You lie in all my many Thoughts, like Light,
> Like the fair light of Dawn, or summer Eve
> On rippling Stream, or cloud-reflecting Lake.
> And looking to the Heaven, that bends above you,
> How oft! I bless the Lot, that made me love you.

A Priest's First Mass

When I was aged about fifteen, the church magazine announced that there would be a coach going from the parish to the cathedral for the ordination of the curate to the priesthood. Now, my grasp of churchy things at that age was rather slim, and I remember being mystified. "But if the curate isn't a priest," I asked older members of the congregation, "what is he?" I only knew that we had a vicar, and that he was assisted by the curate. All this talk of priests went over my head.

The parishioners tried to explain that the curate was something called a deacon, and that he would be ordained priest, because there were certain things that only a priest could do, and that was how it was done in the Church of England. Well, it was hardly a textbook explanation, but it sufficed.

So, off we all went to the cathedral, were given poor seats, could not see a thing, and at the end our curate, who had been a deacon, emerged smiling, now a priest of the Church of God.

One of the things I remembered from that first ordination service I ever attended was a rather strange incident towards the end, when we were all returning to our seats after receiving Holy Communion. A rather mousy-looking woman in a beige raincoat tried to slink out of the cathedral. As she approached the door, the dean of the cathedral appeared running down the side aisle to stop her, his robes billowing out behind him. As he drew near, he shouted out "Consume that, consume that!" My vicar later explained, with a degree of embarrassment, that the lady was a rather unlikely looking satanist. She had received Holy Communion in her hand but, instead of consuming the host, the Body of Christ, she was trying to smuggle it out of the cathedral for their own dreadful satanic rites. This was the first inkling I had as a teenager that being a priest was not all about shaking hands smilingly in the church porch and eating cucumber sandwiches on the vicarage lawn, but that priests sometimes had to deal with some very difficult and fraught situations.

Other Christian denominations, such as the Church of Scotland, English and Welsh Nonconformists, and continental Protestant churches, have *pastors* and *ministers*. The Church of England has bishops, priests and deacons, the same as the Roman Catholic, Eastern Orthodox and Oriental Churches. During the events known as the English Reformation, which really lasted from about 1533 until the Restoration of the Monarchy in 1660, the Church of England wobbled about a bit—some people would say that wobbling about a bit is one of its endearing hallmarks—and ended up by being *not* an entirely Protestant body (which, of course, some people, like the Puritans, would have liked), but as a reformed catholic Church, a subtle but significant difference. The Church of England claims in its formularies to be the historic Catholic Church of this land, cleansed of unscriptural accretions and medieval legends, but in all things in perfect continuity, not just with the Church established by Saint Augustine, but with the very first Christians, who, in the words of one scholar, had probably conveyed stories of Jesus Christ to these foggy islands by the autumn of the year of the crucifixion.

I am rather proud to belong to a Church which has its historic origins, not in the turmoil of the sixteenth and seventeenth centuries, but in the very first days of Christianity. One of the ways in which we may observe this continuity is in the Church of England's three-fold ministry of bishops, priests and deacons. This has its origins in the late first century AD and emerged from much the same melting pot that gave us the New Testament documents: some things, we might say, were passed on by word of mouth, thought about, and then written down. Other things were passed on, thought about, and repeated.

Bishops are the successors of the twelve apostles. We may see the apostles adding new members to the apostolic college, through prayer and the laying-on of hands, in such documents as the Acts of the Apostles and some of the Epistles. All modern bishops can trace their origins back, through the laying-on of hands, to one of the original twelve.

We can also see in the Acts of the Apostles the appearance of the first deacons. In order to free the Apostles, so they could concentrate on their work of preaching the gospel and celebrating the sacraments, deacons were chosen and ordained to help with practical, pastoral work.

During the late first century AD, we may observe the beginning of a further development in the early Church. As Christianity spread rapidly around the Mediterranean and beyond, there were simply too many new Christians for the bishops by themselves to cope with. And so, little by little, we see the gradual appearance of a new sort of Christian sacred minister, the priest. The bishops began to select some of the deacons, and to ordain them with prayer and the laying-on of hands to be priests; and to these priests they would entrust a little of their apostolic authority, to preach the word and celebrate the sacraments. Thus gradually emerged the three-fold ministry of bishops, priests and deacons, which by the end of the first century and start of the second century AD was spreading throughout the whole Christian Church. As I say, the three-fold ministry had its origins in the same melting pot from which emerged the New Testament and we hold it to be the will of Christ for his Church.

And so, today, we greet our new priest, Giles, who is about to do what is at the heart of the priestly ministry and celebrate the Eucharist, which will tie us into the sacrifice of Christ at Calvary and make present the Lord's sacramental body and blood upon the altar, to feed and nourish us with the very life of the Saviour himself.

I am very glad that the day on which our new priest is to do all this is the feast of the Apostles Peter and Paul. The liturgical colour is red, for this is the day when, according to tradition, the two men were martyred in AD 67, Peter by crucifixion upside down, and Paul by beheading.

They were a pretty unlikely pair: Peter, the fisherman, weak and wobbly, who denied Christ three times before the cock crowed; Saul, later known as Paul, the highly intelligent persecutor of Christians, who ultimately came to share their faith in the risen Christ, and used his formidable intellectual gifts to teach and spread the good news. Neither, at first glance, strikes us as very suitable to be apostles; and yet, they went on to be pillars of the Church. The point is that they were called by God to their work and ministry; and, through their opening of themselves to the Holy Spirit, were enabled to do great things for God.

People sometimes say to me, "Why did you choose to be a priest?" The honest answer is that I did not choose to be a priest: God chose me.

Tonight, we see before us Giles, fresh from his priestly ordination. We might think that Sunday 27 June 2010 was the defining moment in his life. In fact, the day of Giles' ordination was but a stage on the journey. Long before he was born, long before he was conceived, Almighty God had always planned that Giles would be a priest in the One, Holy, Catholic and Apostolic Church of his Son Jesus Christ. Little by little, as Giles grew up, the Holy Spirit was at work inside him, whether he knew it or not, preparing him for the moment when he came to acknowledge and accept his vocation from God. It is absolutely vital that all priests know that they have been called to this ministry by God Most High. The Church deliberately makes the process of selection and training long and arduous. There are occasional mistakes, and a few people without vocations are sometimes ordained, while some people with genuine vocations are turned away; but for the most part the Church gets it right.

Once you recognize that God has called you, and your calling is also confirmed by the Church, there is no turning back. You *have* to be ordained, and you have to keep on throughout the rest of your life on earth, doing your level best for the Lord. You could not live with yourself if you shirked it.

The currency with which the priest has to deal on a daily basis is comprised of things such as faith, kindness, goodness, forbearance, forgiveness, cheerfulness, hope, and all these sometimes in the face of great suffering and adversity. These are not things which rate highly in the lives and decisions of high-powered City businessmen, figures in the mass-media, or indeed many people in the street. Yet they will expect to find them all in their priest. At times we priests must be fools for Christ, be taken for a ride, while quietly hoping that, even if some people think we are mugs, Christ may somehow still shine through. Of course, the priest may never be aware of some of the most important things he does or says in his ministry. For instance, Giles, by faithfully getting on with his work over the next three decades, will surely be used by God to help others to realize their own vocations.

In the ordination service, the congregation is asked if they will support their new priest, and they answer in the affirmative. Although that question and answer are part of a ceremony, they are not merely a ceremonial action. The people of God make a solemn promise to God to support his priests. He will want to know on the Day of Judgement how they have fared. No priest is perfect, just as no parish is perfect. We are a group of people called by God to journey together through life on earth at a particular moment in time. We are to support one another and bear each other's burdens. You will be surprised how little support your clergy receive from the institutional Church of England. They deal quietly with some very tragic and complicated circumstances, of which many people in a parish probably know little. Please pray for them and surround them with your active love.

To Giles and my fellow priests, I say: let us remember our calling. We did not choose God; no, he chose us, and appointed that we should bear fruit, fruit that will last. The temptation for any priest is to be so busy with the things of God, that we neglect God himself. Let us pledge to persevere at the life of prayer.

Above all, let us, priests and people together, renew our devotion to Jesus Christ in his Blessed Sacrament. We see our brother Giles do tonight that which defines the priest: celebrate the Holy Eucharist. He stands at the altar, *sacerdos alter Christus*, the priest as another Christ: it will be Giles' hands that take the bread and wine, Giles' lips that say the sacred words, but in very truth, it will be Christ's hands and Christ's voice which consecrate the holy sacrament and offer the holy sacrifice. We pray for Giles, as he does for the first time tonight what God has always wanted him to do, and what he will do thousands of times again, and in many different circumstances, in the years ahead.

And we pray for ourselves, priests and people all, that we may listen out for the voice of God, the God who called Peter, Paul, Giles, you and me. May we open our hearts ever wider to the Holy Spirit, that we may trust and obey, going wherever he would have us go, doing whatever he would have us do.

2 4

The Blessed Virgin Mary

*Preached during the Anglican pilgrimage to the
Sanctuary of Our Lady of Grace, Nettuno, Italy*

It may come as a surprise to some of you to discover that I was once a very pious evangelical young man. I have changed a good deal during the course of my Christian pilgrimage, and I expect that under God's guidance I will continue to change in the years to come.

Thinking back to the evangelical Anglican parish church I attended as a boy and young man, I have much for which to be immensely grateful. Church life was vigorous. The congregation contained some very kind and loving people, who were smilingly tolerant of an inquisitive boy asking lots of questions and who helped me greatly on my Christian journey. Here, I acquired a love and fascination with Holy Scripture which has stayed with me ever since. I was also introduced to the *Book of Common Prayer*, which again had a big impact on me.

Looking back over the years, however, I recall that, apart from a mention at Christmas, the figure of the Blessed Virgin Mary was largely absent from our spiritual outlook, prayers and worship. The vicar and congregation would probably have said that the veneration of Mary (of which they had little direct experience) was unnecessary and might detract from our worship of her divine son, Jesus. At the time this seemed perfectly normal; but with hindsight I think it was somewhat unbalanced. They were *good* people, though, and I am profoundly grateful to God for them.

Aged seventeen, I struck up a friendship with a wise old Anglican nun whom I met in St Paul's Cathedral, Sister Joyce Mary of the Society of St Margaret at Haggerston. I corresponded with Sister Joyce for many years, and, indeed, as a priest I later ministered to her on her deathbed when she was aged one hundred. Sister Joyce helped me enormously in my Christian journey, patiently dealing with my many questions about Christianity with a firm Edwardian hand. I slowly found myself embracing a more catholic and sacramental Anglicanism.

In one of my letters, I asked Sister Joyce about devotion to the Blessed Virgin Mary, which I had experienced in the sisters' chapel but which was new and unfamiliar to me. In her reply, which I have never forgotten, Sister Joyce wrote: 'Mary is not easy to get to know.' She flits through the Gospels. Sometimes we see her clearly; on other occasions we just sense her presence.

Under Sister Joyce's guidance and supported by her prayers, I found myself, aged nineteen, going for the first time to visit the Shrine of Our Lady of Walsingham in Norfolk. Some years later I went on pilgrimage to Jerusalem and the Holy Land. Standing in the Basilica of the Annunciation in Nazareth, looking down at the site where the Angel Gabriel is believed to have appeared to Mary, her vital role in the drama of our salvation was powerfully brought home to me. Not for nothing did the early Church call Mary the *Theotokos*, meaning the *Mother of God*.

The Christian veneration of Mary, I have discovered over the years, leads us to a deeper understanding of what I shall call the 'Christ-event', and to a more rounded and well-balanced understanding of Christianity. I suggest that Mary is significant for three main reasons. Firstly, Mary did what no one else has ever done: she gave something to God, her own body and flesh. I think it was John Henry Newman who said that had we seen Mary and Jesus walking along a street in Nazareth, we should have thought "a mother and her son", because the two would have closely resembled one another. We may picture Mary caring for Jesus as any mother cares for her baby, cleaning him up when he was sick, drying his tears, encouraging him to walk and talk, teaching him to pray, telling him some of the stories of the Jewish people from the Hebrew scriptures, and, with Joseph, taking him to the synagogue in Nazareth and to the temple in Jerusalem.

Secondly, Mary constantly points people to her son Jesus. One of the reasons Mary is so hard to get to know is because she directs our gaze *away* from herself and *towards* her son. She showed him to Elizabeth at the Visitation, to shepherds, to magi, to Simeon and Anna in the temple, to waiters at the wedding at Cana, prompting Jesus' first miracle of turning water into wine. After Christ's resurrection and ascension, Mary is believed to have lived with St John the Apostle, perhaps at Ephesus. It is fascinating to speculate that in her old age, Mary may have told the tales from long ago of Jesus' birth and infancy, and the story of how she and Joseph lost Jesus when he was a boy during a pilgrimage to Jerusalem and later found him asking questions in the temple; which may possibly help explain how these stories found their way into the New Testament.

Thirdly, Mary furnishes us with a supreme example of faith and trust in God and his good purposes: "Here am I, the servant of the Lord," she said at the annunciation, "let it be with me according to your word." To us, she repeats her words from the wedding at Cana: "Do whatever he tells you."

It is no coincidence to discover that, for the most part, the sidelining of Mary began in the sixteenth and seventeenth centuries, and is associated with north European Reformation schisms, which occurred for many reasons, not all of them entirely wholesome. Churches established by strong personalities with grievances tend mostly to have little place for Mary's gentler witness to her son. As Bishop Robert Ladds said so eloquently, we all have our histories, both churches and individuals. We cannot run away from our history, but we need not let ourselves be chained down by it.

Our task, it strikes me, is to find ways—gentle ways, as befits Mary—to witness to the place of Mary in Christianity. I have come to understand that as Christians we are supposed to invite Jesus to fill our hearts and minds, and we should also be conscious of the wonderful work of the Holy Spirit. But we should also seek to reserve a little corner somewhere in our hearts for Mary. I could wish that my fellow Christians who do not consciously have much of a place for Mary in their theology and prayers might make the same journey of discovery as I did, and see how the veneration of Christ's mother enriches our understanding of the incarnation and makes such a difference to our conscious, personal relationship with Jesus Christ himself.

And who knows, in dealing with one bad aspect of Christian history, we might find ourselves liberated to deal with one or two others. Churches coming to appreciate Mary, and to enjoy thereby a richer understanding of Christianity, *may* find it easier to get over other ancient differences and to seek the Church unity that is the will of Christ, who prayed that we all might be one.

Sister Joyce was quite right all those years ago. Mary is *not* easy to get to know; but it is worth persevering. In the end, without detracting from Jesus Christ as some fear, we discover that we have developed a great and affectionate *fondness* for Mary.

2 5

Saint Benedict

11 July

We all have favourite film stars, singers, writers, artists and so on. If I were asked for my favourite saints, near the top of my list I would put St Benedict, whose feast day falls on 11 July. Benedict was born in Norcia around AD 480 to wealthy Italian parents and had a sister called Scholastica. Benedict's parents sent him to Rome to be educated, but he was appalled by the rowdy and licentious behaviour of the students. Aged about twenty, he left Rome and went to live on his own at Subiaco, where he devoted himself to a life of prayer. With time, Benedict's reputation for holiness drew other Christians who wanted to share his way of life. After about twenty-five years he moved to Monte Cassino and established a monastery there. He died here in the chapel aged sixty-seven and was buried in the same grave as his sister.

While at Monte Cassino, Benedict compiled the book for which he is most famous, the *Rule of St Benedict*. Consisting of seventy-three short chapters, Benedict describes it as a 'little rule for beginners'. The rule suggests how to organize a Benedictine monastery, but more than that, it says a great deal about how to be a Christian; so much so, that it has always been read and followed by Christians outside monasteries whose vocation is to be married, or parents, or to serve God here in the world.

The first thing you notice on reading the *Rule of St Benedict* is that it is Christ-centred. The aim of everything is to encourage Christians actively and consciously to seek Jesus. The Rule is also very biblical, with quotations from the holy scriptures in nearly every sentence. The way of Christian life advocated by Benedict is even tempered, humane and well balanced. It has been described as 'sanctified common sense'. After the Bible, the *Rule of St Benedict* was probably the most influential book in Western Europe for a thousand years, and its influence can even be detected in the 1662 *Book of Common Prayer*.

In the rule Benedict looks at three principal aspects of leading a Christian life: prayer, relationships, and work. In the Old Testament it says 'Seven times a day shall I praise thee', and so Benedict decreed that his monks should come into the chapel seven times during the day for services, which principally meant singing the Psalms and reading the Bible. They got through all 150 Psalms every week. They also were to have periods of private prayer each day, though Benedict is careful not to prescribe what form this should take. This regular round of prayer each day was the backbone to everything else they did, sustaining all their activities, helping them deal with all their problems and develop their vision.

Benedict also spent much time writing about relationships. He pictured the monastery as a family, with the abbot as the father of the community. But religious communities are just like other groups of people: there are problems, personality clashes, people have illnesses, get ratty, become ambitious, are tempted and fall into sin. Benedict writes about how to deal with this, and indeed how to seek Jesus through all these things. Remember, too, that monks and nuns may have been unmarried, but traditionally they knew all about child rearing because they taught children, and—though it might sound a bit barbaric to us—people would sometimes bring children to the monastery and give them to the community to be brought up. Mumps, measles and teenage awkwardness were all part of the Benedictine experience, as much as middle age, old age, illness and death.

Between their services and prayers, Benedict's monks worked. I have mentioned children, and education was a big part of monastic life. Benedictine houses frequently contained schools; in the Middle Ages, many Benedictine monks studied and taught at Oxford and Cambridge, and at universities across Europe. Before printing, books were painstakingly copied by hand in monasteries, which contained large libraries.

Another large part of monastic work was gardening and farming: the community had to feed itself. Benedictine monks played an important role in the development of agriculture, and incidentally the production of champagne was perfected by a French Benedictine, Dom Perignon. Benedictine monasteries also housed some of the earliest hospitals— St Bartholomew's Hospital in London was founded by Rahere, a Benedictine—and the care of the sick has always been an important part of their work. St Benedict does not see any contradiction between any of these working activities and the life of prayer. Quite the reverse: rightly understood, he sees them as all ways of worshipping God. If any of the monks are asked to do something which they think is beyond their capabilities or strength, Benedict encourages them to explain carefully why they feel unhappy about it. If they are still asked to do it, he urges them to get on with the work, trusting in God to give them strength to accomplish it.

I suppose we might sum up Benedict's vision of an ideal Christian life as one that is fully integrated. Jesus is to be sought and served every moment of every day, from getting up until going to bed. Faith is to be lived out, not confined to the mind. We might fear that this would lead to religious fanatics, yet Benedict's Rule, by contrast, has enabled millions of Christians down the ages to grow into happy, well-balanced people.

Benedict's vision is in contrast to two common ways of life amongst contemporary churchgoers. Some people seem to go to church to escape from the rest of their life. Certain forms of worship can, frankly, be escapist; and this can be found in all traditions, charismatic, Anglo-Catholic, and liberal-modernist. But Christianity is not about disappearing into a religious Disney-world for an hour once a week, and then carrying on in a very different frame of mind from Monday to Saturday. It is, instead, about finding and serving God here and now.

Secondly, some people say "Oh, I'm under so much pressure. There are the children, the house and the garden to look after. I work long hours, and my job is very stressful. I'll try to come to your services occasionally, if I can." Well, I too have worked in an ordinary job and commuted by train to the City every day, and I entirely sympathize and understand how tired one can become. But to this second approach, St Benedict suggests that if we re-evaluate our lives and priorities, and spend more time in prayer, and indeed go to church every Sunday, we shall cope better with the stress and all the other things. When we spend time with Jesus Christ, we open ourselves to receive his love and power. We shall not receive Christ's sacramental grace if we stay away from Christ's sacraments. St Benedict also teaches that we should try to view our commuting, or cutting the grass, or the school run, as part of our worship. One of his great ideas is *conversatio morum*, the conversion of life. Not only are our minds to be converted to Christ, but our bodies and our whole way of life.

I was given my own copy of the *Rule of St Benedict* in 1983 by Dom Damian Sturdy OSB, a monk of Prinknash Abbey, and I have read it almost every day since. It is put together to allow you to read a little paragraph every day. As I said, many people have found the *Rule of St Benedict* helpful, whether they are called to the monastic life or to live in the world. Today, as we give thanks for St Benedict, may I commend his *Rule* to you, as a valuable aid to leading a Christ-centred, integrated, Christian life.

2 6

Saint Frideswide

19 October

Preached at St Stephen's House, a theological college in Oxford

Just in case Sister Benedicta Ward happened to be with us in church,[12] I thought it prudent to look up St Frideswide in her excellent book *Miracles and the Medieval Mind*. There, I discovered that the legend of St Frideswide states that she was an eighth-century Anglo-Saxon princess and the founder of a religious house in Oxford. In a twelfth-century history, we read that Frideswide was promised in marriage by her father to a king's son. She, however, preferred the religious life and fled, pursued by her enamoured suitor. He, poor man, was struck blind in answer to her prayers—nice girl! Upon abandoning his claim of marriage, the suitor's sight was miraculously restored, and Frideswide went on to establish her religious community. Following the translation of her relics in 1180, Frideswide's tomb became a centre of pilgrimage and healing. So, allowing for medieval accretions and embellishments, what we have here is the tale of a young woman, who overcame some difficulty to abandon her old life and embrace the cloister.

What can St Frideswide tell us as we seek to follow Christ in the altogether changed conditions of our own century? Indeed, a further question: what are saints, and what are they *for*?

The answer, I suggest, can begin to be found in the Lord's Prayer, in particular, in the words: *Thy kingdom come, thy will be done, on earth, as it is in heaven.* What is the kingdom of heaven like? It is the realm where God's sovereign will is carried out, perfectly, entirely, marred by no sin.

We can in some measure anticipate this by seeking to know and fulfil God's will for us here on earth. *Thy will be done, on earth, as it is in heaven.* Saints like Frideswide are followers of Christ who, for one reason or another, are recognized by their fellow Christians as people who have *especially* managed to fulfil God's will here on earth, and thus in their lives they have reflected something of God and his love to those around them.

The point of festivals like St Frideswide's day is that they remind us (a) that we, too, must seek God's will, and (b) that this is necessary for our lives and ministry. I sometimes say to couples I am preparing for marriage that I want them to go off and say a little prayer: "Lord Jesus, am I doing the right thing? Do you want me to marry this person to whom I am engaged? If you do, please take away all my nerves as the wedding day draws near. If you do not want me to marry this person, please send me a whacking great rocket!" They usually look at me as though I am completely mad. It has never occurred to them that the Lord of heaven and earth, the creator of all things and giver of vocations, has anything to do with their choice of a marriage partner. And yet, how could you possibly marry someone if you knew that God did not want you to?

In a few weeks, some of you will begin visiting parishes and looking at curacies. In a few years you will begin looking at incumbencies. You will have many considerations to bear in mind. Is the vicar all right? Can you cope with the worship or music? Perhaps you have elderly parents to whom you must be near, or children for whom you must find suitable schools. All these are very important. But far more important is a little, simple question: 'Lord Jesus, what do *you* want? Do *you* want me to come here?' There would be little point pulling strings to become a vicar in Mayfair, if deep down you knew that God wanted you to go to Bethnal Green. Or indeed, vice versa.

Someone once asked Archbishop Michael Ramsey how we knew God's will. "Well," he replied, "you get a sort of a hunch." I think that is right. There are a few things we can bear in mind when we are seeking God's will.

For a start, will a particular decision or course of action lead us *away* from ourselves and *towards* other people? If the answer is "yes", then the Holy Spirit is probably guiding us. If a decision is taken solely to help or advance ourselves, then it is at least doubtful. Remember, traditional depictions of hell always include a bishop who has bought or manipulated his way to high office.

Similarly, the Holy Spirit never contradicts himself; so, he will not lead us to do something which is contrary to the broad tenor of Christianity down the ages.

If, when we see an avenue opening up before us, we can see both good and bad, but it still feels right to us, that avenue is potentially the right one for us to take. If we can see only good, or only bad, perhaps our vision is clouded, or the Holy Spirit is urging us to think again.

The lives of the saints show us that not infrequently they suffered for their faith. There are plenty of people, even within the Church, who have their own personal agendas, and seeking God's will does not seem high on their list of priorities. There are problems and challenges in all our lives, and at times fulfilling God's will is far from easy or comfortable. But we know that, if we are faithful, God will always get us through, even if it is only by the skin of our teeth.

For myself, I would say that there is one great advantage to going to the parish to which you sincerely believe God wants you to go. When all is going wrong, when you have an awful PCC meeting, or the flower ladies are arguing over who forgot to order the Easter lilies, you can say in your prayers, "Well, Lord, *you* wanted me to come here: *You* sort it out!" I am a bit cheeky here—because, after all, it maybe *we* ourselves who need sorting out—but it is a great comfort to know that we are where we are supposed to be.

Similarly, despite the problems and difficulties we sometimes encounter in priestly ministry, when we try to do God's will, we often experience a sense of peace, knowing that we are in safe hands. If we feel persistently wretched about a course of action, we must think again. Not long after I came to my present country parishes, I was offered a living with the freehold in a smart market town. I was put under a great deal of pressure by the patrons, churchwardens and my fellow clergy to accept. But I felt increasingly uncomfortable and even had trouble sleeping. I tried convincing myself, and made lists of reasons why I should go there; but in the end, as I was having my breakfast one day, I thought "How often does God have to tell me not to go?" I telephoned the patron, explained that it was not right and withdrew my candidacy. Immediately, I felt as if

I had shed a great weight, and a blanket of peace descended upon me. A short while later some problems surfaced in my present parishes of which I had previously known nothing, and which I then had to deal with. But I sensed that I had heard the voice of God telling me not to move, and that he wanted me to stay where I was, to try to bring some healing and encouragement to those affected.

I have harked on at some length about seeking God's will. The saints were just men and women like you and me. They were not all of one type or personality, but of all types. They have lived in every part of the world, in all conditions. The common denominator is that they carried out God's will, whatever that was for them. They had come to realize that when we say *Thy will be done* and mean it, we are cutting through that which is seen and temporal, and focusing directly upon that which is unseen and eternal. We tune in to ultimate reality. God's will alone endures, and in carrying it out, the saints have found wholeness, peace and joy.

Frideswide, the Anglo-Saxon princess turned nun, and all the other saints, stand in heaven, beckoning, waving and encouraging us. They call upon us to fulfil God's will, to feed his sheep, and in so doing, to grow into the men and women God has always planned and wanted us to be.

2 7

The Queen's Diamond Jubilee

*Preached in Thaxted Parish Church in 2012 to members of
the Order of St John of Jerusalem and St John Ambulance*

Today, we have come together as the family of St John in Essex to give
thanks to God for our Order's Sovereign Head, Queen Elizabeth II, who
this year has reigned over us for sixty years. This is only the second
diamond jubilee in British history, and so is a very rare and historic
occasion.

I think that all boys and girls, and probably most men and women,
have wondered what it would be like to be king or queen for a week or
two, and have imagined that it might be rather fun. I daresay it would.
But after that, I think we might discover that being the monarch is harder
work than we had envisaged. And, of course, there is no retirement.

We are all familiar with the public aspect of the Queen's role:
Trooping the Colour, the state opening of Parliament, the Cenotaph on
Remembrance Sunday, and so on. But such events are only a very small
part of the daily work of the Queen. For the most part, Her Majesty's work
goes on quietly, regularly, largely unseen. Think of the famous red boxes
containing state papers which the Queen needs to read or sign, even on
holiday. Then there are mountains of daily correspondence. The Queen
is sent a daily digest of events in parliament and sees her prime minister
once a week. All sorts of people are received by the Queen in audience,
week after week, throughout the year.

To each and all the Queen has a word. I was once sent by the Bishop
of Portsmouth to attend a course at St George's House, a study centre
in Windsor Castle. One free afternoon, I went for a walk, searching out
second-hand book shops. Around 4 o'clock I thought I would treat myself

to a cup of tea and piece of cake. The tea shop was very busy, and three people asked if they might sit at my table. I said they were most welcome, and so a middle-aged couple helped in a very elderly man with a chest full of medals. He had just been received by the Queen in Windsor Castle, and I think she may have presented him with an award of some sort. As the man sat there, describing it all to his friends, his kindly old face lit up. I remember him saying, "She was so easy to talk to; just like talking to my neighbour next door." That old man is probably long dead now, but at the end of his life, a conversation with the Queen made all the difference. He knew he was valued and appreciated. Only the Queen, I suspect, could have done that; and in much the same way only the Queen could have carried out such a healing tour of Ireland last year.

When the Queen was crowned in Westminster Abbey in 1953, the prayers, investiture and crowning, and especially the anointing with holy oil, made it plain that being our Queen is a Christian vocation. *Vocation* is a key concept. Our primary Christian vocation is just that, to be Christians: men and women, boys and girls, who share our lives and love with Jesus Christ. After that, Jesus gives each of us our own personal vocation—a way of life in which we are to serve God and the men and women around us. Some people are called by God to be married, others to be single. Some people are called to be priests, or monks, or nuns. The Queen's very special vocation is to be our Queen. And our vocation, as members of St John, is to save lives and to care for the sick and suffering, and that is a high and noble vocation.

Now, in St John, we know all about bodies and the way in which all the different parts fit together and work together. It is exactly the same with our vocations. In St John, we need ambulance drivers, first aiders, and instructors, and people to write the letters and pay the bills. None is more important than the other—all fit and work together—and we all need one another.

The same is true in the wider world, as we seek to serve God and his people. All our individual vocations fit together, like a big jigsaw puzzle. Today, we give thanks to God for the way in which our Queen has fulfilled and continues to fulfil her vocation and gives us all an example of service to follow.

Great Britain has changed enormously since the Queen came to the throne. The Queen has adapted the monarchy down the years to cope—sometimes with a bit of tweaking, sometimes with rather larger changes. And yet, you could say that today the Queen is doing exactly the same sort of work as her father King George VI and as her grandfather King George V. The circumstances, and perhaps more importantly the human needs, have changed, but the monarch's role is the same. I think we could say that the same is true of St John: from time to time we have to adapt how we do things, to take account of changing needs and circumstances and improved medical resources, but our core tasks are unchanged and unchanging: to save lives and to care for the sick and suffering.

As I have gone around our county as your chaplain, visiting members of St John on duty at events such as the V Festival and the Clacton Air Show, I have been immensely impressed both by everyone's professionalism, and also by their cheerfulness. The people to whom we minister are a cross-section of society. Sometimes they are pleasant and grateful. Sometimes they are drunk and rude. Most commonly, they are upset or worried. I have found it very moving to see how they are always treated politely and with respect by our St John staff. I should like to offer you all my personal thanks and warm admiration.

I also want to offer you an insight about care of the sick which I have gained through my years of priestly ministry. When people are sick and suffering, they are, in a strange way, especially close to God. They may themselves not be aware of it, but it is nonetheless true. When we care for them, if we look with the eyes of faith, we can sometimes see a reflection of Jesus Christ in them.

The reverse also is true. Jesus went about healing the sick. He is the inspiration of our Order, and we wear his cross as our badge. When we care for the sick, the sick may catch a glimpse of Jesus and of his love for them in our words and deeds. The gospel may be written, as it were, on our faces, in our hands and actions. For the sick, and for those of us caring for them, it can be a life-changing experience.

So today, to our Queen, we offer our homage and loyal congratulations as she celebrates her diamond jubilee.

To God, we offer our prayers and thanksgiving for our Queen's reign, and for her wonderful example of a Christian vocation, faithfully lived out.

And to each other in St John, and to the men and women to whom we minister, we renew our personal commitment to serve the sick and suffering, *Pro Fide et Pro Utilitate Hominum,* for the Christian Faith and for the Benefit of Humanity.

The Week of Prayer for Christian Unity

*Preached in the Roman Catholic Church of
the Holy Spirit, Great Bardfield*

Perhaps we might begin by asking ourselves the question: why do we need to have a Week of Prayer for Christian Unity?

We all know what a millennium is: one thousand years. It is not long since we began the third Christian millennium. In the first Christian millennium there was just The Church: you could receive Holy Communion in Iceland or Egypt, Portugal or Byzantium and still be in the same Church. There were differences of course—different forms of service, different emphases on aspects of prayer and spirituality, a wide variety of schools of theology—but it was all within the one Church.

In the second Christian millennium, it all started to unravel. In 1054, there was the Great Schism between East and West which resulted in what we would now call Roman Catholicism and Eastern Orthodoxy. In the sixteenth century, there was a complex series of events in different countries which have become known to us as the Reformation, when splits developed in the Catholic Church in Western Europe, leading to the establishment of Lutheranism, Calvinism, Presbyterianism and, in England, Anglicanism. From the seventeenth century onwards, there were splits in England, when more Protestant-minded Christians, unhappy with the Church of England's blend of reformed catholicism as opposed to full-blooded Protestantism, separated themselves and formed what later became known as Nonconformist chapels: Baptists, Congregationalists, Methodists and so on.

These events took place for a whole variety of reasons. Some of them were honourable. At times, parts of the Church have become unbalanced, have placed too much emphasis on some aspects of Christianity and not enough on others, and there has been a need for internal reform. But there have also been darker motives at work: power-struggles, politics, dynastic ambition, economics and, in England, snobbery and disdain between church and chapel. Then there have also been sins: pride, hardness of heart, ambition, a refusal to forgive or be reconciled, and the portrayal of Christians from other Churches as bogeymen.

You might say, then, that in the second millennium we have made a real mess of things. Instead of internal reform with charity, we have had revolution, schism and hatred amongst those who claim to follow the same Lord Jesus Christ.

The Week of Prayer for Christian Unity developed in the twentieth century as a way of reminding Christians of all denominations that a divided Church is not the will of Jesus Christ, that we should freely acknowledge our errors, and work and pray for reconciliation and unity. There are, I would suggest, two reasons why we should work to merge all our Churches into one Church. The first of these is theological. When, please God, we get to heaven, we shall find that there is only one Church: one, holy, catholic and apostolic. We will not be greeted by angels directing us like traffic policemen: "Catholics straight ahead, Orthodox to the right, Anglicans to the left, Free Churches over there." No, we shall all be one family, with one God and Father of us all. The Church on earth is part of the same Church in heaven. If the Church in heaven is united, so the Church on earth should likewise be united, reflecting the unity of the Holy Trinity. We forget that the Church is something sacred, founded by Jesus, a part of the gospel package. It is far more than just a cooperative of like-minded people, and we have done something very wicked in breaking it up.

The second reason why we should work for one Church is a practical one. English society is changing very rapidly. We are, I believe, on the cusp of a very different world, an England where the predominant values are those of secular materialism. The main difference is not patterns of church-attendance, but, more basically, how people reach their decisions. How many people taking a decision—ranging from whether to spend some money to whether to marry a particular person—think of what the Bible says, what the Church teaches, or even say a little prayer asking

God to guide them? Not many. Lives are valued by what you earn, your appearance, where you live, what car you drive, where you have your holidays. I have seen a few snatches of the television programme 'Essex Wives', but in the end I turned it off because—apart from finding it pretty dull—I was saddened by the lives of the participants. They were living solely in the here-and-now, with no glimpse of the Eternal, no idea of the difference Jesus Christ can make, not much to hold on to when life gets tough, or when we are confronted with our own mortality. That, I fear, is how many people in England live their daily lives.

From the Churches' point of view, many of our congregations are top-heavy in terms of age, and I expect that the coming years will see us squeezed to the margins of national life and culture. Now, I am not bothered about power and influence for the Church—I have always felt we should be standing alongside people rather than dominating them—but I *am* troubled about the prospect of a country where most people have no idea of the gospel, and no glimpse of the love of God in their lives.

If I am honest, I fear that the task of re-evangelizing English society is beyond the Church of England as it is presently constituted. I suspect it is beyond the Roman Catholic Church in England and Wales acting alone, or the Methodist or United Reformed Churches acting alone, and so on. But I begin to have a fuzzy vision in the back of my mind of a different Church re-emerging in a century—or two or three—which might evolve and bear powerful and effective witness to Christ. It would have to be a very different Church for a very different world, and above all it would have to be a reunited Church. Like that of the first millennium it would need to be big enough to include a variety of views and practices when it came to secondary things, but be one over the core doctrines of the faith. A Church that is truly One, Holy, Catholic and Apostolic.

The Week of Prayer for Christian Unity traditionally ends with the feast of the Conversion of St Paul on 25 January. This is a very helpful image. Saul the slayer of Christians was transformed into Paul the apostle of Christ. We read in the Acts of the Apostles that something like scales fell from his eyes after his conversion. Paul had to turn around, begin again and lead a completely different way of life. We Christians must follow this pattern if we are to be true to our Lord. We shall have to concentrate on what really matters in the Christian life and be clear about what is of secondary importance. There will have to be sacrifices, though that is nothing new to those who follow him who was crucified for our sake. We shall, above all else, have to try to stick close to Christ in prayer and consciously seek his will for us.

You might say that all this is a bit highfalutin for a few Roman Catholic and Anglican country parishes; to which I would reply that we can still pray for Church unity, manfully face up to our differences, and share as much as we possibly can here and now. The world desperately needs the gospel, and the Church will best serve both its Lord and the people entrusted to its care if it struggles to overcome ancient divisions and bring about the unity that is Christ's will.

We cannot go back to the first Christian millennium, but we can try to ensure that the third millennium is not like the second.

2 9

Requiem for a Churchwarden

Preached at the funeral of Mrs Gillian Morrell

I have heard it said that teachers—or at least, good teachers—are born and not made. In the case of Gill, I can well believe that is true. When did the idea of becoming a teacher first enter her mind? I am afraid I am not sure. Was it when she was growing up in Sutton with her parents Tim and Irene and her sister Carole? Or perhaps at Girton College, Cambridge, where she read Greek and Latin? Gill had a very distinguished academic career; she taught Classics in St Paul's Girls School, Leytonstone High School for Girls, Forest School, Mossbourne Academy, Hackney, and until last term, New Testament Greek to ordinands at St Mellitus College. But, as I said, *good* teachers are born, not made, because anyone can simply impart knowledge. But there is much more to being a good teacher than that. Gill, if I can put it this way, had the gift of standing alongside people, listening—she was a good listener—encouraging, drawing out skills and abilities. Anyone can teach enthusiastic pupils. Gill was very good at standing alongside those who were struggling, or who doubted their own abilities, or who perhaps had illnesses or problems at home that were affecting their work.

Now, in your imagination, leave the classroom for a bit, and reflect on the rest of Gill's life. We see her doing exactly the same to so many other people. Chris told me he simply adored Gill; and Helen and Jeremy have spoken to me of how they loved their mother with all their heart and soul. I think, without exception, we all valued Gill hugely, and grew as human beings through our friendship with her. Yet, I have to add, she was no pushover. If something was wrong, she would make it plain—but always very tactfully. I knew that sentences beginning "Now look, Father

Robert, dear . . . " usually meant that I had done something daft, or was being unreasonable, or missing the point. Sometimes all three.

One of Gill's friends spoke of her great gifts of forgiveness and of not being judgemental. I certainly observed that. "Yes," she might say to me of some high-up person in the Church of England, "they are being very stupid over that; but just let it go." I learnt much from Gill about the importance of trying to *enmesh* a parish church in the local community; and the importance of taking risks, and sometimes doing things that were messy or untidy, because they were the *generous* thing to do; and we worship a God who is, above all, generous.

Gill, to state the obvious, was very generous with her time and gifts. I would ring her sometimes and ask "What have you done today?" "Well," she would say, "I went to Ealing to see my aunt, then I saw someone else in London on the way back, and I caught the train to Chelmsford where I taught New Testament Greek to the ordinands, and now I'm just finishing off something at my desk in Great Bardfield." That was not untypical. Did you know that Gill was involved with the Christian Message Service, recording short two-minute Christian messages of help and encouragement which people could telephone and listen to? Then there were all her little notes and letters, keeping in touch and encouraging people. In our village of Great Bardfield she was involved in all sorts of ways in the local community, and especially Great Bardfield Historical Society, of which she was the secretary. Gill wrote a book about religion in Great Bardfield: typically, she went to great pains to ensure that she got the theological terminology correct. She also worked very hard to commission two blue plaques for the village. From further afield, many people will have met Gill when she accompanied Chris to Royal Air Force Cadet events over the years.

Inevitably, Gill's illness and death have shocked and distressed all of us. It was my privilege to administer the Last Rites to Gill. Typically, her last words were of love for Chris and her family, and of thanks to the hospital staff. And yet, we deeply feel her loss. I want to say quite plainly today that it is all right to feel a bit sad—you are not letting the side down. Jesus said "Blessed are they that mourn, for they shall be comforted." And he knew what he was talking about. Grief is part of love, and no love is ever wasted or lost.

I must confess I was quite surprised that last Sunday afternoon in the hospital when Helen said to Gill, "You've enjoyed being churchwarden, haven't you?"—and Gill nodded vigorously several times. Gill, like all churchwardens, had to cope with some pretty difficult problems and issues. Several times she told me she had had sleepless nights worrying about things; which in a sense reassured me, because I had had sleepless nights too. Gill used to say, "Life, you couldn't make up the script!" I must say I enjoyed having Gill as churchwarden, with her great resources of humour and common sense; and I found that she was someone upon whom I could try out ideas. If they were good ideas, they were encouraged; if they were bad, I was usually told "I wouldn't do that—no." She was also quite good at pulling my leg; and I would pull hers in return. Bats in the church were a frequent bone of contention. I thought they were horrible, with all their droppings everywhere. Gill thought bats were *wonderful*. After they had been particularly messy, usually around Harvest time, I would explode: "Right, that's it, I've had enough—I'm going to shut all the doors and poison the lot!" "Oh Father Robert", Gill would reply, "you don't mean that." "I do!" "But they are all God's creatures." The bats and their mess, I regret to say, remain.

Needless to say, Gill did lots of other things in St Mary's as well as being churchwarden, including masterminding our Sunday School, sorting out rotas, helping with the Christmas bazaar, church cleaning and candle changing.

At this point, I want to make it plain that her involvement here was not the same as someone who, say, was deeply involved in a sports club or political party. Gill's involvement with St Mary's was not an end in itself; she did not do so much just for the parish church, but for the Owner of the church, by which you will understand I do not mean the Bishop of Chelmsford, but Jesus Christ, the Son of God. Her busyness in the service of the Church, alongside her care for people, was an outward expression of her deep inner faith in Jesus.

For many years Gill attended an Anglican parish in London, until there were some very upsetting problems at that church. She then went to Cambridge Park Methodist Church in Wanstead. Moving to Great Bardfield, she discovered us, and returned to the Church of England. Gill would frequently tell us of the Methodist Church and say "Oh, they do such and such, and it is so much better than the Church of England", and usually she was right. But, spiritually, it was a bit like living abroad and then coming home. You bring your continental experiences with you, but you also sometimes appreciate things at home more than you did before. So it was with Gill: I think she came to appreciate more greatly various aspects of the Church of England and its liturgy and spirituality. It was her wish that she should have a Requiem Mass. The Mass, the Eucharist, Holy Communion—whatever you want to call it—has many aspects and layers. One of the things it does—rather like baptism—is to link us in with the Easter story. At the font we are grafted into the Easter story; and at the altar we renew that loving link and commitment; we are with Christ on Good Friday, as he offers his life in sacrifice for the sins of the world, and we are with the womenfolk on Easter Day, finding the tomb empty, for Christ has risen, having defeated sin, death and evil. We talk to God about these things in the Eucharist and link ourselves to them.

Archbishop Lang used to say that when we die, we pass out of sight. But of course, because we pass out of sight, we do not pass out of existence. God has given us life, and he does not take it away. Gill has gone on before us; and today, through the medium of this Requiem Mass, we accompany her with our heartfelt prayers and very real love. Our first reading was chosen by Gill and speaks to us of God's love. Gill is now experiencing that love in all its fullness: God is raising her up like Jesus, forgiving her sins, healing her wounds, sorting out bad memories, and fitting her for heaven. And we who are left journey on, along the same road as Gill, inspired and fed by her memory and example, and no doubt aided in the Communion of Saints by her prayers. Let the last word be from the first Letter of St John. In a sense it is a message to us from Gill, who chose it for us: "Beloved, let us love one another, because love is from God; everyone who loves is born of God and knows God."

3 0

The Rededication of a War Memorial

St Katharine's Church, Little Bardfield

It was something of a historical accident that the First World War ended at 11 o'clock on 11 November 1918. The prime minister, David Lloyd George, had instructed the British representative at the Armistice negotiations in the forest of Compiègne, Admiral Sir Rosslyn Wemyss, that the fighting was to finish at 3 o'clock. Lloyd George wished to stand in the House of Commons, produce his watch, and be the first to announce that the war was over. He hoped that he would be cheered to the rafters and that he could make political capital out of it, with an eye to the post-war general election.

Admiral Wemyss was not very happy with his instructions. He realized that if the war dragged on for a few more hours than was necessary, hundreds of people might be pointlessly killed or maimed. Also, the poetry of the eleventh hour, of the eleventh day, of the eleventh month appealed to him. Disregarding the prime minister's orders, Wemyss suggested that the Armistice should begin at 11 o'clock and the French and German representatives agreed.

Wemyss hurried back to Paris. Fearing, quite rightly as it transpired, that he had landed himself in hot water with the prime minister, he decided to bypass Lloyd George and contact King George V, the Commander-in-Chief. Using the rudimentary telephone system of the day he managed to be put through to the King in Buckingham Palace. The King and his equerries then telephoned the government ministers and the service chiefs to announce the news of the Armistice at 11.00 a.m. on 11 November 1918.

How, I wonder, did the news of the Armistice reach Little Bardfield? Did someone have a telephone? Did anyone walk or cycle from Thaxted? Did someone receive a telegram? The news reached most places during the morning, and the villagers would at last have realized that the worst war in the history of mankind up until that point was finally over.

The First World War—the *Great War* they called it—affected every community, almost every family. There had been nothing like it since the English Civil War in the seventeenth century. Of the men from Little Bardfield who went off to the First World War, only one returned home afterwards; the rest lost their lives.

Edward Mears	George Gunn
Walter Marsh	Alfred Drane
Filmer Spicer	John Perry
Walter Sams	William Coe
Herbert Stock	Thomas Perry
Ernest Coote	George Cowell

Why did they join up? Well, some perhaps went for a laugh or to escape boredom. But many men volunteered—and remember it was a volunteer Army until 1916—for the highest and noblest of motives.

Because of Adolf Hitler and the Nazis, we have tended to overlook just how dangerous was the militaristic and ambitious Germany of Kaiser Wilhelm II. The German Empire desired, economically, politically and militarily, to dominate the whole of northern Europe, at the expense of France and Russia. As German troops invaded Belgium and France in 1914 and sought a swift victory at almost any price, stories began to emerge of their use of 'deterrent terror' to repress the civilian population. This involved acts of brutality, the deliberate destruction of property, deportations, and the murder of civilians including women and children. After the First World War, some people suggested that these reports had been black propaganda by the Allies. Recent historical research has shown that they were often true.

Now, not all German troops were brutal, but some were, and this, together with events such as the German introduction of asphyxiating gas and the sinking of the *Lusitania* in 1915 had a huge impact upon the British population. Bishop Winnington-Ingram of London spoke of the mother who told him how her son, startled by newspaper accounts of German atrocities towards women and children, exclaimed, "They shan't do *that* to Mum and Sis!" and rushed from the house to the nearest recruiting office. We may well surmise that many of the men of Little Bardfield who went off to the Great War did so to protect those they held most dear.

What of those who were left alive on the evening of that Armistice Day? What of the families who could hear people outside cheering and lighting bonfires on Armistice night, but who found it hard to celebrate because they had lost a much-loved son, or husband or father? In at least a dozen houses in Little Bardfield, life would never be the same. They were left with a lifelong sorrow.

For many people, the evolution of the rituals of the Armistice, the Flanders poppies, the wreaths, the Two Minutes' Silence, proved in a strange way to be a great comfort. They were a way of channelling grief and of providing mutual moral support on each 11 November.

In Little Bardfield, the villagers clubbed together in the early 1920s and commissioned a war memorial. It is a great pleasure today to see it skilfully restored to its original glory by Stephen Bellion.[13] War memorials are significant, because for many people they became surrogate graves. Perhaps their loved ones had no known grave or, if there was a grave in France, they could not afford to visit it. And so the war memorial was cherished and for ever associated with the memory of those who had made the supreme sacrifice. It is interesting that a small village like Little Bardfield commissioned such an elaborate and beautiful war memorial, which really would not seem out of place in a regimental chapel in a cathedral, and which must have cost a great deal of money. This, I suggest, tells us much about the grief that was a daily part of so many lives in the years after the Armistice.

I think, too, that it is significant that they chose to erect their memorial inside their parish church. St Katharine's is an ancient church, nearly a thousand years old. It is a sermon in stone. It points us beyond ourselves, to things unseen but eternal. By erecting their war memorial inside the church, the villagers of Little Bardfield were explicitly associating the twelve men listed upon it and their own grief with the Christian Faith.

Not for nothing, I suspect, does the monument rest upon two angels, God's messengers and watchmen, and the *Chi-Rho*, the Greek emblem of Christ.

At the heart of the gospel of Christ lies the mystery of Easter. Jesus Christ, the Son of God, came to earth to bring us God the Father's love and to offer us salvation. But humankind did the worst thing imaginable: we rejected Christ, condemned him, and put him to death on a cross outside Jerusalem on Good Friday.

On Good Friday, though, something was going on which was invisible to the human eye. Jesus Christ, dying on the cross, offered his life in sacrifice to God the Father, to take away the sins of the world and to defeat sin, evil and death once and for all. God accepted that sacrifice. Three days later on Easter Day, Jesus rose from the dead in the resurrection. The worst thing that could happen, did happen; and God still loved us.

The death and resurrection of Christ is the lens through which we Christians look at the world and try to make sense of it. Easter reminds us that the world is not the way God wants it to be; but it reassures us that God is ultimately in charge, and that if we will but have faith in him, all shall be well in the end. For the Christian, death is not the end, but a step on the journey; and if we love and trust Jesus, God the Father will grant us a resurrection to eternal life just like that of his dear Son.

And so we come here today, not to celebrate war and killing people, for war and killing are both evil and stem from the Fall. Nor do we come to gloat over former enemies and rake over long-past atrocities, for the past is in the hands of God, and our task is to work for reconciliation and friendship amongst the nations.

Instead, we come here to remember twelve ordinary men who went forth for the highest and noblest of motives, to defend liberty and all they held dear. They did not ask to die, but because they did, we enjoy certain freedoms. One of those freedoms, of course, is freedom of religion. Today we honour and salute their memory. We pray that we, each in our own way, may learn from their selfless example. We commend them and ourselves, into the hands of the Son of God, who died upon the cross and rose again three days later, thinking of each of them, and also of each of us.

Harvest Thanksgiving

I remember running into the house when I was a small boy and shouting out, "Mum, I'm *starving*!" Does it ring any bells? It is a common expression; but, mercifully, most of us have never seen anyone who is actually starving. Recall, if you will, some of the film and photographs of prisoners in Belsen and the other Nazi concentration camps after their liberation in 1945. That is what starvation looks like. The last time there was a danger of starvation in Europe, surprisingly, was as recently as 1991. The Communist regimes had collapsed in Eastern Europe, and so had their agricultural production. They managed to avoid the worst, but only just. I remember one Harvest time organizing a massive collection of bags of flour, sugar and rice, which the poor churchwarden and I had to lug to a central receiving centre, to be sent on to Romania.

Harvest thanksgiving in churches as we know it today dates from the 1840s. For three years there were bad harvests in Great Britain and Ireland. Some 21,000 people starved to death and many others barely got enough to eat. Finally, there was a good harvest, with food enough for all. Queen Victoria asked the Privy Council to arrange for prayers of thanksgiving for the harvest to be offered to God in all churches and cathedrals. And here we all are, some 180 years later, still coming to church to thank God for the harvest.

I offer you three harvest-time thoughts to take away and ponder.

Firstly, food is precious. Food waste is therefore a waste of something very important. As a nation, we throw away vast amounts of food every day. What, I wonder, could we each do to cut down on waste?

Secondly, although we may be spared the sight of people starving to death, there are still many people in Great Britain who do not get enough to eat. This is deeply disturbing and raises all sorts of questions.

I am pleased that we have taken the decision to collect food at the back of church for the food bank. It would be good if we all took the trouble to buy one or two tins of something really nice—not some old rubbish from the back of the cupboard, but something good we would like to eat ourselves—and popped them into the basket. If that made someone smile and think that life was still worthwhile, we should have done something valuable.

Thirdly, a reflection. The other day, I visited my parents. The motorway was closed, so I drove back the country way. I was very moved by how beautiful all the fields looked after the harvest, with autumn colours beginning to appear. Then—change of gear coming up—the other night, I had to squash a mosquito: it was him or me! I do not like killing things, even mosquitoes—and as I wiped him up with a piece of paper and consigned him to his grave in the bin, I mused "What a work of art is a mosquito"—such a tiny but perfect creature. Then I thought of the fields I'd seen, and of the trees, and of you and me.

How wonderful is the world God has created: like a big jigsaw puzzle, with everything fitting in together. Yes, it is messed up by the Fall and Original Sin. But there is still much that is deeply wonderful. God has given us the precious gift of life on earth. From the very first second of our conception, the Holy Spirit is busy, working in and through us, infusing us with God's love. Probably the best way we can celebrate the harvest is to make the most of our time on planet earth, allowing God, who carefully creates so much, carefully to shape and fashion each of us as he knows best.

A Visit to the Relics of Two Saints

Recently I had to attend a meeting at Church House, Westminster. Getting there rather early, I thought that I would stroll down Victoria Street to Westminster Catholic Cathedral and visit the relics of St Thérèse of Lisieux which were on temporary display there.

As I approached the cathedral, I saw a crowd of people. Turning the corner into the square, my heart sank. There, patiently queuing to get in, was a long crocodile of several thousand people. "How long is the wait?" I asked an official. "About an hour and a half," he replied, "but priests on their own can go straight in." I walked forward and soon found myself standing in the nave. About halfway down was a domed glass container, with the reliquary inside.

Now, we are not much accustomed to relics of saints in England. We used to be, if you go back far enough, but they have become unfamiliar to us. Having said that, I visited a house in Perthshire earlier this month where I saw two little boxes containing the hair of Bonnie Prince Charlie. Relics of a different sort, I suppose; it is only a question of degree.

Relics belong to a pre-photographic age. Sometimes they may be actual bits of a saint—bones or hair—or they may be things that came into contact with a saint, such as fragments of cloth. They are tangible aids to recollection. When we see the relics, we look beyond them, as it were, to the person himself or herself. We are put in closer touch with them. We see an ordinary man or woman, pretty much like ourselves, who became a saint. Beyond that, we see God himself. In venerating a saint, we are praying to become a little bit more like that person in our own lives. We hope that as God transformed the saint with his grace, so he will pour the same grace into our lives and help us on our Christian pilgrimage.

Back to Westminster Cathedral at lunchtime last Wednesday. Do you know the thing that surprised me about it all? I was struck by the sheer ordinariness of everything. As I have said, there were several thousand people outside the cathedral, and about another thousand inside. They were of all ages and backgrounds. Many carried flowers. In the centre of the nave were a group of nuns who cared for the sick. Some people arrived in wheelchairs. A son pushed his old father. There were no obvious religious eccentrics. There was no hysteria. No one moaned or shrieked. The crowds slowly came forward, in a very good-humoured way. As they got to the relic, some touched it with their hands, others placed a flower at the base, most paused briefly to say the prayer that had been forming itself in their minds as they queued.

And then, it was all over. They went out into the sunshine. And yet, I am sure they were slightly changed people by their experience. In the life of prayer, much goes on at a very deep level inside us, of which we are never aware. There is a message here about finding and serving God in the ordinary things of life.

I went on to my meeting, where, incidentally, I heard that the Archbishop of Canterbury was to visit the relics of St Thérèse the following day. I then made my way to Westminster Abbey for a Sung Eucharist for the feast of St Edward the Confessor. It marked not the anniversary of his death, said the dean, but the day of the translation of his relics into Westminster Abbey. The service was very good, with an excellent sermon. At the end, we were told that if we wanted to, we might go behind the high altar to pray at the tomb of the saint-king, whose relics are still inside. I did not think many people would go, but there was a sudden flurry of movement, and several hundred people formed a queue. When I got to the tomb, I discovered that you could kneel in one of six little niches right underneath the tomb and say your prayers. In my little niche, someone had left two red roses.

Not bad, I thought, as I made my way home, two saints in one day. They could not have been more different people. One was a nineteenth-century French nun, who saw her mother die and her father become insane, and who died tragically young of consumption, saying that she wanted to spend her time in heaven doing good on earth. The other was an old Anglo-Saxon king, who ruled wisely and justly, and sought to glorify God by the way he exercised his kingship.

What was the common denominator, I wondered, as I boarded the train home? The answer, for Thérèse and Edward and for us, was the sheer attractiveness of holiness and the things of God. The devil, as William Booth once observed, seems to have all the best tunes; and it is surprising how attractive we find sin and evil, until we succumb and find they have turned to dust, ashes and guilt. But, holiness and the things of God? Well, once we have managed to look at them, we find that they are attractive too, indeed, just that wee bit more attractive than sin and evil, despite the devil's blandishments. When we see that which is good and holy, we find that, at a very deep level, it is what we want for ourselves and for all whom we love; for, in the end, we realize that this is all that ultimately matters.

In venerating relics and celebrating the lives of saints, we are actually celebrating the work of God. We open our hearts afresh to God, and, as he transformed Thérèse and Edward with his grace, we pray that he will change us too, as he sees fit.

3 2

Christ the King

Cast your minds back to the feast of the Epiphany on 6 January, when we celebrated the journey of the Magi to worship the Christ Child in the stable at Bethlehem. You will recall that after their long journey, they produced gifts for the infant Jesus, each of which tells us something very important about him: *frankincense*, which symbolized Christ's role as our high-priest, and *myrrh* for a sacrificial victim. But it is the significance of the Magi's first gift that I want us to think about today: *gold* for a king.

Today, we celebrate the feast of Christ the King. "Funny sort of a king," you might say, "I thought he was a carpenter from Nazareth." You would be right, for Jesus was a carpenter from Nazareth; and yet he was also the King of kings and Lord of lords.

We can see two very important signs of Christ's kingship in the events of Holy Week. Firstly, Jesus' entry into Jerusalem on Palm Sunday was strongly reminiscent of the coronation procession of a new Hebrew king. At the start of their reign, Jewish monarchs rode through the streets of Jerusalem on a donkey, the royal beast, to be crowned and anointed in the temple. The crowds would shout "Hosanna" as their new king passed by, and they would put carpets on the ground for the donkey to walk upon. Jesus rode through Jerusalem on a donkey on Palm Sunday, the crowds shouted "Hosanna to the Son of David", and they put clothes upon the ground for his donkey to walk upon. Like the Jewish king, Jesus made his way to the temple. But here, instead of being crowned and anointed, the evangelists Matthew, Mark and Luke tell us that Jesus cleansed the temple by overturning the tables of the money-changers and setting free the sacrificial pigeons that were for sale; an event, among others, which led the Jewish authorities to decide that he must be killed.

Secondly, five days later Jesus was crowned in Jerusalem, not with a crown of gold placed reverently upon his head by a priest, but with a crown of thorns jammed into his flesh by a mocking soldier. His throne was the cross, upon which he, the king, died for his people.

Here we see what sort of a king Jesus really is: a king after a heavenly pattern, not an earthly one, and one who said, "My kingdom is not of this world." He is a king who shows us that much of what we think is important is actually insignificant or even misguided. He is a king who teaches us that "anyone who wants to be first must be the very last and the servant of all". This is not an easy message to get across, and not always easy to live by, and it is very different from many of the values of the world around us. And yet, we are called to live in this world and to bear witness to Christ the King.

One childhood memory that sticks in my mind is the evening when my parents and I were walking along a street in London and we saw Princess Alexandra. My father was wearing a hat, which he removed straight away as a sign of respect. Princess Alexandra might only be a fairly peripheral member of the Royal Family—albeit a very nice one—but she is still royal, and such a small courtesy was appropriate.

Now, if it is appropriate for us to show courtesy and respect to relatives of our earthly Queen, I suggest that we should also show every courtesy and respect to those who are relatives of Christ our King; in other words, to everyone who has been baptized. I would go further and say that we should also show courtesy and respect to those who have not been baptized—perhaps they have never had the opportunity—and also to those of other religions, or of no religion, even if we disagree with them. Christ, after all, died upon the cross for all. But, I also want to suggest that courtesy and respect, unless they are backed up with genuine concern and real help, are a bit meaningless. St James expresses it in his own blunt way in his Epistle:

> If a brother or sister is naked and lacks daily food, and one of you
> says to them, "Go in peace, keep warm and eat your fill," and yet
> you do not supply their bodily needs, what is the good of that?
> So faith by itself, if it has no works, is dead.
>
> *James 2:15–17*

Today is the last Sunday of the Church's year. Next Sunday is Advent Sunday, the beginning of a new year for the Church. By appointing this feast of Christ the King for today, the Church intends that we should end the year gazing firmly into the eyes of Jesus Christ, as a reminder to us of what is really important. At the end of our lives, the only thing that will matter is whether we have loved the Lord our God with all our heart, mind, soul and strength, and our neighbours as ourselves. We cannot truly claim to love the Lord we have never seen if we do not love the brother or sister we can see.

The feast of Christ the King reminds us of what—or rather, who—ultimately matters. It also poses a question for us: does Christ *truly* reign in our hearts and lives as King?

Notes

1   Robert Beaken is the author of *Cosmo Lang, Archbishop in War and Crisis* (Tauris, London, 2012). Archbishop Lang's words have popped up from time to time in his sermons.

2   Betjeman, John, "Christmas", *Collected Poems* (London: John Murray, 2006), p. 155. Reproduced by permission of Hodder and Stoughton Limited.

3   In the Septuagint or Greek translation of the Hebrew scriptures, "I AM" is ἐγώ εἰμι (*ego eimi*). In Exodus 3:14, the story of God speaking to Moses, we read: καὶ εἶπεν ὁ Θεὸς πρὸς Μωυσῆν λέγων· ἐγώ εἰμι ὁ ὤν. καὶ εἶπεν· οὕτως ἐρεῖς τοῖς υἱοῖς Ἰσραήλ· ὁ ὢν ἀπέσταλκέ με πρὸς ὑμᾶς. (God said to Moses, "I AM WHO I AM". He said further, "Thus you shall say to the Israelites, 'I AM has sent me to you.'" NRSV). [My emphasis].

4   John 18:5: ἀπεκρίθησαν αὐτῷ, Ἰησοῦν τὸν Ναζωραῖον. λέγει αὐτοῖς Ἐγώ εἰμι. (They answered, "Jesus of Nazareth". Jesus replied, "I am he." NRSV). [My emphasis].

5   John 14:6: λέγει αὐτῷ Ἰησοῦς Ἐγώ εἰμι ἡ ὁδὸς καὶ ἡ ἀλήθεια καὶ ἡ ζωή· οὐδεὶς ἔρχεται πρὸς τὸν πατέρα εἰ μὴ δι᾽ ἐμοῦ. (Jesus said to him, "I am the way, and the truth, and the life. No one comes to the Father except through me." NRSV). [My emphasis].

6   John 8:12: Πάλιν οὖν αὐτοῖς ἐλάλησεν ὁ Ἰησοῦς λέγων Ἐγώ εἰμι τὸ φῶς τοῦ κόσμου · ὁ ἀκολουθῶν ἐμοὶ οὐ μὴ περιπατήσῃ ἐν τῇ σκοτίᾳ, ἀλλ᾽ ἕξει τὸ φῶς τῆς ζωῆς. (Again Jesus spoke to them, saying "I am the light of the world. Whoever follows me will never walk in darkness but will have the light of life." NRSV). [My emphasis].

7   John 10:11: Ἐγώ εἰμι ὁ ποιμὴν ὁ καλός ὁ ποιμὴν ὁ καλὸς τὴν ψυχὴν αὐτοῦ τίθησιν ὑπὲρ τῶν προβάτων ("I am the good shepherd. The good shepherd lays down his life for the sheep." NRSV). [My emphasis].

8   Hebrews 4:15: the Greek word πεπειρασμένον, depending on the context, may be translated as having been 'tested' or 'tempted'. The New Revised

Standard Version has chosen 'tested', with a footnote offering 'tempted' as an alternative. I prefer 'tempted'.

9   Matthew 4:1–11.

10   Dix, Gregory, *The Shape of the Liturgy* (London: A. and C. Black, 1982), p. 774.

11   Greene, Graham, *Monsignor Quixote*, (London: The Bodley Head, London, 1982), pp 46–8.

12   Sister Benedicta Ward SLG is a sister of the Anglican religious Community of the Sisters of the Love of God at Fairacres Convent, Oxford. Sister Benedicta is a theologian and historian of early Christian spirituality, and a Supernumerary Fellow at Harris Manchester College, Oxford.

13   Stephen Bellion Church Art.

Lightning Source UK Ltd.
Milton Keynes UK
UKHW021939040520
362766UK00009B/716